The Voice of the Child

If we want children to be successful, confident, independent learners, we need to relearn the skill of truly listening. *The Voice of the Child* builds on a number of theories which recognise the importance of interacting with, and listening to, the children in our care, and demonstrates how these can be put into practice – listening, communicating and hearing the voice of the child effectively.

The book addresses each phase of a child's development, from birth through to five years, and explains how communication skills can be used to support individual children's specific needs. Chapters offer practical tips and strategies to help early years practitioners to listen and communicate in such a way as to encourage and enhance the development of a child's speech and language skills. With case studies and reflective questions included throughout, the book highlights the importance of listening to children in order to keep them safe, ensure they feel included in their community and to promote their confidence and self-esteem.

The Voice of the Child is essential reading for early years practitioners and students, including those on Childhood Studies courses, who want to gain a clear understanding of how their own communication skills can impact on the child. It is also valuable reading for parents and families as their interactions are vital for a child's development in speaking and listening.

Julia Maria Gouldsboro is an Early Years Consultant and Lecturer for the Foundation Degree in Early Years at North Hertfordshire College, affiliated with the University of Hertfordshire, UK.

The Voice of the Child

How to Listen Effectively to Young Children

Julia Maria Gouldsboro

Routledge
Taylor & Francis Group

LONDON AND NEW YORK

First published 2018
by Routledge
2 Park Square, Milton Park, Abingdon, Oxon OX14 4RN

and by Routledge
711 Third Avenue, New York, NY 10017

Routledge is an imprint of the Taylor & Francis Group, an informa business

© 2018 Julia Maria Gouldsboro

British Library Cataloguing in Publication Data
A catalogue record for this book is available from the British Library

Library of Congress Cataloging in Publication Data
A catalog record for this book has been requested

ISBN: 978-1-138-63616-3 (hbk)
ISBN: 978-1-138-63617-0 (pbk)
ISBN: 978-1-315-20614-0 (ebk)

Typeset in Optima
by Cenveo Publisher Services

Contents

Acknowledgements

Many people have been supportive and helped me to complete this book. My sincere thanks to them all.

I would particularly like to thank Routledge for their kindness and support, with special mentions for Clare Ashworth, Elsbeth Wright and Aiyana Curtis.

Thank you to Ciara Gouldsboro for illustrating the book with photos from a local setting and thanks to Carole Spraget, staff, parents, families and children of Buxton Bears pre-school in Chingford, north east London. They welcomed me into their wonderful setting and shared their positive practice with me.

A warm thank you extends also to Carmel Burke and Clair Louise Walsh for demonstrating how the voice of the child can be expressed so many ways through the hundred languages of children, such as music, movement and yoga.

A sincere thank you to the families that have added their thoughts on development. Thank you to Ciara and Ciaran Halpin and their wonderful family Darragh, Jack and Emma; and a sincere thank you to Gemma and Matthew Stanway, their wonderful son Thomas and their supportive family, Peter and Jan Stanway, John and Jan Walsh, Ollie, Adam and Claire-Louise, who have helped me explain the development of the child through some lovely personal reflections.

This book is dedicated to all children that they will have a voice that is listened to and respected as they grow up and be part of conversations and communication that enable them to view the world in a positive light.

Finally, I would like to thank my children Ryan, Conor and Ciara for the many wonderful conversations we have had over the years that will forever be my happiest memories.

Introduction

The voice of the child

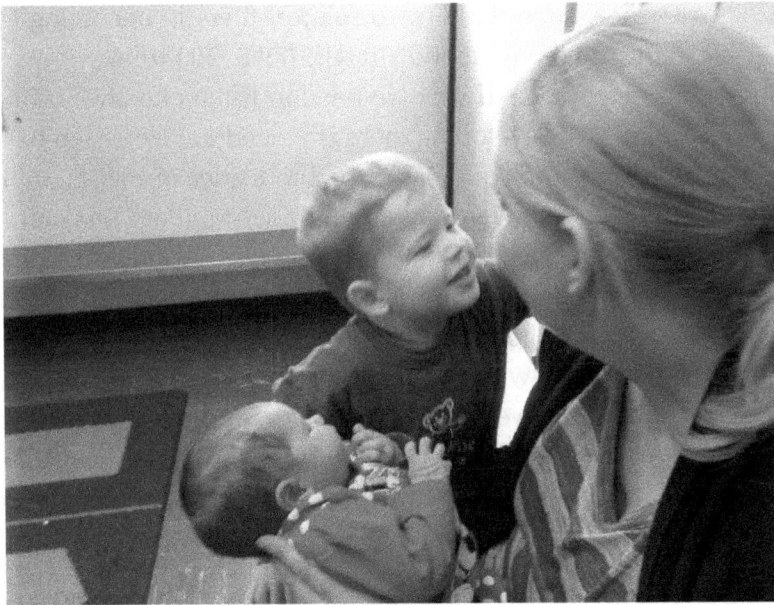

Carla Rinaldi is an advisor to the Reggio Emilia approach and explains the voice of the child succinctly. She states that listening ultimately gives a sense of value and respect to the other person (Rinaldi, 2001: chapter entitled 'Documentation and assessment: what is the relationship?').

The verb 'to listen' conjures up many meanings that lead to a successful pedagogy of listening (ibid.). If we want children to be successful independent learners, we need to relearn the skill of listening.

Theorists and philosophical approaches place great emphasis on speech and language being an essential component to knowledge and understanding for a young child, helping them to have a clear sense of the world around them. 'Babies and young children make sense of their world in many ways, including use of all their senses and their whole being' (Riddall-Leech, 2005: 91). This exploration enables them to become competent learners 'ready, eager and able to learn' (DFE, 2014b: 5).

Speech equips children to access the world. Every child, from a very young age, has a voice; essentially, we need to listen to that voice. From the cries of a baby at birth when they take their first breath, children are expressing their needs and feelings. Parents learn to decipher the different meanings of the cries of their babies and practitioners learn the skill of listening to each child's needs, wishes, thoughts and feelings. This does not mean giving the child whatever he or she may demand, but it does mean listening and responding in a way that further progresses their understanding to support them in becoming 'capable, confident and self-assured unique individuals' (DFE, 2014b: 6).

This book considers how and why we need to listen effectively. First, when children are learning and developing there is a need to take a step back, learn to pause and wait to encourage them to be the leader in that learning. Children need time to process thoughts and their understanding. This comes about through effective listening. Understanding the ages and stages of developing communication skills and knowing how to support all children ensures each child's needs are met. Furthermore, children have the right to participate in decision-making and in the wider community from a very early age.

This book describes how we can value children's opinions as participants in the decision-making process. It means allowing them to be involved in decisions and participating as a valuable member of their community. It examines how it is extremely important to listen and act upon any concerns that children share with the practitioner, using the correct procedures, with the aim of keeping them safe.

I hope to reflect on the voice of the child and examine why it is important to a child's holistic development. I intend to link theory and legislation to practice and share effective strategies and examples of good practice.

The pedagogy of listening

This chapter introduces the theoretical perspectives that value the importance of listening to children. It will give an overview on how theoretical perspectives and philosophical approaches consider the importance of listening. It will reflect on current thinking and, in relation to speaking and listening, will suggest how to apply theory to practice, enabling effective listening with children in our care to be successful.

Children need to be listened to right from birth

Table 1.1 Key words

Key words	Explanation
Theorist/theoretical perspective	Early years educators can draw on many theories to inform and guide their practice
	Examples include Bruner, Vygotsky and Piaget
Philosophical approach	Philosophical approaches influence play and learning
	Examples include Forest schools, Reggio Emilia approach, Steiner schools and Montessori schools
Legislation	Laws that have a direct influence on education through policies and procedures in settings
	Examples include the Children Act 2004 and the Equality Act 2010
Pedagogy	The holistic way that we teach children and support their development can be described as the ethos of a setting

The 'pedagogy of listening' is a phrase created by Carla Rinaldi, adviser to Reggio Children (Rinaldi, 1983, cited in Clark and Moss, 2011). It underpins a child's social relationships and their relationship with the environment.

Listening involves children and adults using many languages and codes to express themselves. It also involves pauses and turn-taking. To listen means to welcome and recognise different opinions and viewpoints. In addition, it involves listening to something or someone in context; listening demands dialogue. To listen to the voice of the child, a practitioner needs to understand how to listen effectively.

All settings have an ethos, a pedagogical approach that emphasises how they will support children in their learning and development. A pedagogical approach is based on holistic development where a setting has a strong ethos or mission statement about how children under their care are nurtured and how interaction with the child supports development in all areas of learning and growth. Many settings adopt a philosophical approach, such as Montessori or Forest schools, and most settings have foundations in the theoretical perspectives of education.

A summary of theoretical perspectives and philosophical approaches

Theories suggest many ways that children learn and develop in all areas. Below are examples of theoretical perspectives for speech and language, reflecting how theorists enable the practitioner to support the voice of the child.

Noam Chomsky

Noam Chomsky explained that, as humans, we have an innate mechanism built in to us to develop speech known as a language acquisition device (LAD). Chomsky summarised that all children have an instinct to acquire language and suggested that children learn speech even if they have been deprived of a stimulating environment (Berwick and Chomsky, 2016). However, further research into speech and cases such as 'Genie, the wild child' (Rymer, 1994) illustrate that, if adults and peer groups do not nurture speech, it will not flourish or progress.

Genie is a true story of a child that had abusive parents and spent many years tied to a chair with no interaction with the outside world. When discovered, living in terrible conditions, adults supported her by interacting with her and communicating through signs and gestures. They observed how she began to learn vocabulary rapidly, even though she had missed the crucial age when most children acquire it. However, it was observed that her communication and interaction did not develop as well. It would seem interaction with others is vital for language to develop successfully. Jerome Bruner identified this support as the language acquisition support system (LASS).

Jerome Bruner

Jerome Bruner *(1983)* believed that children required a system, namely LASS, whereby they need to hear language around them. This involves the practitioner playing a pivotal role by providing age-appropriate resources and having the skills to encourage young children to learn to read, write and speak. The main factors that support a child in language acquisition are having rich interactions and warm relationships (Daly *et al.*, 2006).

It may be accurate, as Chomsky suggests, that we are all born with an innate sense of language, but it appears that if children do not have positive social interactions, they will not progress in language and speech or know how to use meaningful speech for social interaction. One of the main factors that impinges on language development is when a child has not had opportunities for social interaction at a young age. Bruner described language as central to a child's learning and development. He saw children's cognitive development linked to language and divided the process into three areas:

- *Enactive mode*: understanding the world through senses. Children, from a very early age, learn and develop by exploring through touch, taste, smell, sight and hearing. This is where they build up their vocabulary and descriptions of the environment.

* *Iconic*: whereby children increase their understanding through visual imagery or use items to represent something – for example, a banana may represent a telephone. Children start to make sense of the world and give meaning to objects.

* *Symbolic mode*: children transfer the meaning of pictures or other items. They use language and symbols to make sense of the world – for example, print, signs and pictures.

Daly *et al.*, 2006

Bruner's theory can be useful to language acquisition as the stages can help in supporting the individual stages of children in language acquisition. Some may need more opportunities for sensory play to increase vocabulary; some children may be very quick at deciphering images and visual cues, transferring it into print.

Bruner saw the role of the adult as one that supports a child, 'scaffolding' their learning to enable them to become confident and independent in their development.

The voice of the child is part of genetics, but the role of the adult is essential in fostering the voice of the child. This means that the adult must be a good role model.

Albert Bandura

Albert Bandura described the importance of the adult as a good role model, paramount to children's development. Children watch and learn from each other and adults. This impacts immensely on adults as they need to be good role models for children. His experiment, called the 'Bobo doll', observed children's response to watching adults behaving aggressively towards a toy (the Bobo doll) (1961) (Bandura *et al.*, 1963).

Regarding speech and language, children will pick up words and phrases used by adults and other children. Sometimes this may be inappropriate language. If adults or peers behave aggressively, children may imitate this behaviour. If adults use words that are negative or demeaning, children may copy these words or label themselves as bad or rude. Language is a powerful means for either building up someone's self-esteem or breaking it down. Bandura argues that adults can help children develop positive behaviours and attitudes by 'out-loud' thinking and problem-solving (David, 2004).

Children need opportunities to make sense of their world. They work within a comfort zone, repeating actions and movements, repeating phrases they understand and can link to meaning; then they are ready to move on. The role of the adult is to enable children to progress in their learning. The voice of the child achieves success and development when it is fostered and extended with the support of caring and positive adults.

Lev Vygotsky

Lev Vygotsky considered that children need adults to extend their learning. He called this the *zone of proximal development*. Extending learning relies on observations and knowing the child well to plan for next steps that challenge their capability. Vygotsky viewed language as one of the greatest tools for communicating with the outside world. He saw a link between language and thought. He believed that children needed to talk to adults about everyday experiences and described this as the process of speech (Daly *et al.*, 2006).

Vygotsky: the process of speech

Two years: children use social speech, which Vygotsky defined as external communication, used to talk to others. The role of the adult is vital here as someone who listens and interacts with the child, and who extends conversations by asking questions to recall information from stories shared or experiences encountered.

Three years: Vygotsky explained that children used private speech, which he linked to thought; he explains that thought and language merge. *Private speech* is *speech* spoken to oneself for communication, self-guidance and self-regulation of behaviour. Children from two to about seven years old are usually observed engaging in *private speech*. Although it is audible, it is neither intended for nor directed at others. Vygotsky sees 'private speech' as a means for children to plan activities and strategies and therefore aid their development. As practitioners, this has an impact on our teaching. Children need to use their voice to make sense of their learning. They need opportunities to talk aloud about what they are doing, what they need, how they will achieve their aims, so teachers need to learn the skill of listening and when to interact and when to observe.

Children are not the only ones that practice private speech. Many adults may revert to this skill, talking to themselves through a difficult task or when reading out instructions.

Seven years: Vygotsky explains that children use what he described as silent speech, which enable children to self-regulate their learning. For example,

A treasure basket can 'provide the rich and nurturing environment that babies and young children need if they are to thrive mentally, emotionally and physically' (Hughes, 2009)

we see this in schools when children develop from reading aloud to reading in their heads or calculating addition and subtraction using pens, paper and resources to mental maths (Dolva, 2009).

Practitioners need a clear understanding of development so that they know the general stages children go through. This will impact on the next steps set for children and will ensure practitioners identify specific needs and support children through observations and assessments.

Jean Piaget: stages of learning

Jean Piaget understood development as stages of learning and believed that children need to extend their experiences to achieve learning. This is linked to any area of learning and below is a description of the stages to demonstrate how they are linked to communication and language.

Stages of learning

Birth to two, sensory motor stage: babies use their senses to find out about the world around them. Elinor Golddshmied believed that children use their senses to explore the world. She introduced the *treasure basket* as an example of a heuristic approach to learning, where the child leads their own learning, explores and makes choices.

The forest can create a wealth of learning

Although language may not be vocal, there is a lot of private speech or internalised speech existing as they explore.

Montessori also believed sensory play helps young children make sense of the world and kick-starts the thinking process. The Montessori website describes the child as a 'sensorial explorer' as they study the world through the senses and so make sense of the world (see Montessori Primary Guide, 2017).

Piaget broke down this stage into smaller stages, showing a baby's development as making sense of their own world progressing to realising the wider environment to which they can react to and be responsive.

Example of learning through the senses

Imagine the learning that can take place from a walk in the forest.

Crunching leaves, the different sights in the different seasons, light cast on tree trunks and the pungent smell of fungi. Lifting logs to spy where the insects live and looking at the insect's legs, skin and shape.

The essence of these experiences is captured and conveyed through the colour, sounds, feel, warmth and smells of a child's interaction.

Table 1.2 The stages of development as outlined by Piaget

Sensory motor stage	0–2 years	Sensory play
Pre-operational stage	2–6 years	Symbolic play
Concrete operations	6–11 years	Logical thought
Formal operations	12 years +	Abstract thinking

Two to six, pre-operational stage: children develop thought processes and use symbolic play to make sense of the world around them. Piaget described the child learning to use the symbols associated with language, with the child as egocentric, explaining that a child thinks that everyone sees the world as he or she sees it. He saw children only using speech to make sense of their play and not as a form of communication. The main function of speech at this time is to externalise the child's thinking rather than to communicate with others.

At this stage, he observed toddlers often pretending to be people they are not – for example, superheroes, police officers or doctors – sometimes playing these roles with props symbolising real-life objects. In addition, children felt that toys such as teddy bears and dolls have human feelings.

Six to ten, concrete operations: children start to think on a more abstract level. Piaget saw this stage as the beginning of logical thought. He explained that children start to process why and how things happen and can understand why and how.

Children can conserve concepts to classify and to arrange objects in height or weight order, known as *seriation*. However, Piaget conducted his studies on his own children; his research has been criticised for not taking in to account different cultures.

12+ formal operations: young people can apply what they have learnt to new situations; this is when Piaget believes that children can think in the abstract. This demands a young person to develop skills in listening and analysing and evaluating concepts, demonstrating a clear and detailed understanding.

Philosophical approaches and current researchers

Philosophical approaches and current researchers unify theoretical perspectives and the pedagogy of learning. Many philosophical approaches are active within the Early Years Foundation Stage curriculum.

Friedrich Froebel

Froebel believed that practitioners should encourage self-expression through play and that the outdoor environment was very important. When outdoors, many opportunities open up for listening, touching and smelling the outdoors, which extend vocabulary and language. Froebel used movement, song, rhythm and rhyme to provide key learning experiences (Tovey, 2016).

Anna Craft

Anna Craft described learning as the 'little C' creativity. She explained that when children use their imagination and are encouraged to be original, creativity thrives. She saw creativity as a much wider skill than art, drama or music, including skills of talking to someone, working with others or thinking alone. She considered possibility questions to enable children to problem-solve as enhancing learning and development (Craft et al., 2015).

Vivien Gussin Paley

Vivien Gussin Paley believes that imaginative play and storytelling can help young children make sense of the world around them and develop language successfully (Gussin Paley, 1990). Storytelling can act as a platform for the voice of the child. It enables a child to express themselves, allows them to recreate stories or experiences relevant or of interest to them and it also enables the practitioner to understand the interests of the child. It may be that the practitioner views the choice of superhero play in a negative light, but it has to be appreciated that choice in play acts as the voice of the child and needs to be channelled into a positive experience.

Curriculum

The curriculum demonstrates a philosophical approach to early years education. Curricula around the world that promote the voice of the child include:

1   Te Whariki curriculum, New Zealand
2   Reggio Emilia Approach, Italy
3   Forest schools
4   Montessori curriculum
5   Steiner schools.

The Te Whariki

This is the New Zealand curriculum. Te Whariki means 'woven mat' and describes five strands as essential to development:

1 Well-being

2 Belonging

3 Contribution

4 Communications

5 Exploration.

It considers a print-saturated environment and staff that ask open-ended questions as vital to improving outcomes for children.

Strand 4, communication, sets out goals for children to achieve:

* *Goal 1*
  Children experience an environment where they develop non-verbal communication skills for a range of purposes.

* *Goal 2*
  Children experience an environment where they develop verbal communication skills for a range of purposes.

* *Goal 3*
  Children experience an environment where they experience the stories and symbols of their own and other cultures.

* *Goal 4*
  Children experience an environment where they discover and develop different ways to be creative and expressive.

My ECE Experts, 2013

A setting needs to provide opportunities for the variety of ways that the voice can be expressed.

Montessori

The child's name is one of the most important words to the ears of the child. Spoken language in the Montessori classroom is encouraged by each curriculum area containing language designed to enrich vocabulary. Activities such as focusing on attention or self-confidence develop the voice of the child. Conversation in the classroom is encouraged by opportunities such as a special interest table, holidays and birthdays, projects about different cultures. The children are spoken to on their eye level and listened to through quality interactions with the practitioner.

Reggio Emilia approach

Malaguzzi developed the Reggio Emilia approach, using principles based on the work of Vygotsky and Piaget. The approach believes that all children are communicators; the many ways they communicate are defined as the 'hundred languages of children'. Malaguzzi focused on the role of the adult and positive interaction between adult and child.

The Reggio Emilia approach considers routines highly effective in enabling children to anticipate the day and so reassure them, building up confidence and self-esteem (Thornton, 2014).

Forest schools

Forest schools are designed to ask what the environment can offer to intrigue children and lead them to explore, ask questions, problem-solve and work as a team. It encourages children to manage risks effectively (Knight, 2016).

Steiner schools

The focus is on the spoken word in this approach. Children learn through meaningful experiences and formal education is avoided until the age of seven years. Songs, puppets, stories and movement introduce literacy.

> Its radical principles, based on a view of the human being as composed of body, soul, and spirit, allows for a truly holistic and balanced education that nourishes the whole child. The author explains, in a clear and lively style, many aspects of Steiner's educational theories, especially the three stages of child development and how the Waldorf curriculum provides a healthy understanding, nurturing, and support for these phases.
>
> Edmunds, 2004

Puppets can encourage communication in children

Theoretical perspectives and philosophical approaches

The impact of many theoretical perspectives and philosophical approaches demonstrates the main factors for successful language acquisition. There are a number ways that theories affect practice and below is a list that identifies factors that practitioners need to understand and demonstrate for an effective and successful voice of the child to flourish.

1   Understand the stages of development
2   Give children time
3   Build quality interactions with children. Show them right from the start that we have a genuine interest in them
4   Listen completely
5   Be positive role models when using language with children
6   Work in partnership with parents
7   Provide a sensory curriculum for the very young
8   Value a child's home language

1   Understand the stages of development

First, by understanding the various theories as summarised above, practitioners are enabled to realise that children follow a pattern of development. However,

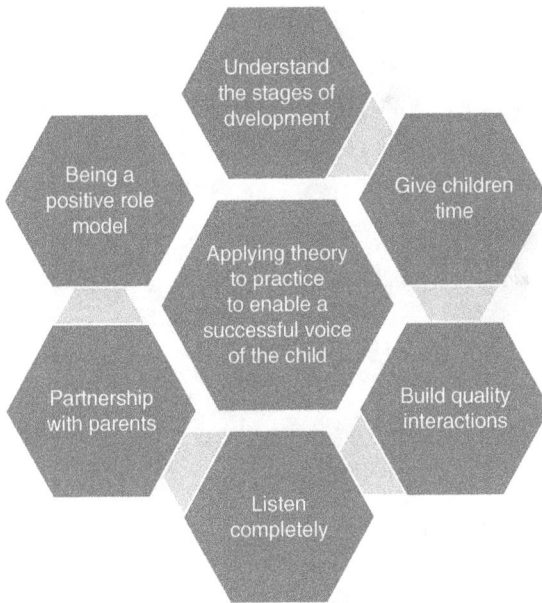

Figure 1.1 Applying theory to practice to enable a successful voice of the child

it needs to be understood that children develop at different rates, but usually in the same sequence. Every child is unique and so the development will go at the pace of the child. Also, development is holistic. While focusing on communication and language, other areas will also link in to the development of speaking and listening.

Children come from many different cultures and circumstances and this may affect opportunities that they are given to develop. The stages of development as outlined by Bruner and Piaget demonstrate that young children need many opportunities to play and explore. Abstract concepts are learnt from a foundation in play experiences. This has an influence on the curriculum that is organised for children.

2   Give children time

Theoretical perspectives also demonstrate that children need time to pass through these stages. Many will need more time than others will; many may be more ahead in the stages of development. The art of conversation may come very easily to us as adults, but children are juggling many parts of speech and language. One of the key points to remember is that children need time to express themselves. Vygotsky emphasised how important it is for children to have time to process their thoughts. They use words to help them make sense of their environment and they need to choose words or sounds that can be easily interpreted.

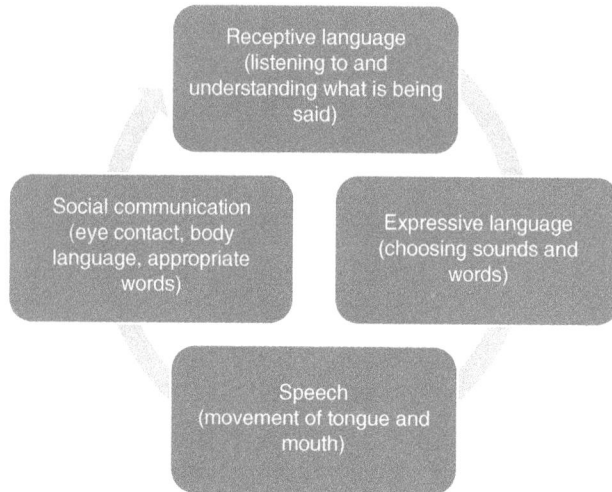

Figure 1.2 Ways of supporting children when expressing language

They need to understand the mechanism of their mouth and tongue to form the speech (Lowry, 2013). This all helps to support them in being competent communicators. Practitioners need to take a step back and listen. They should allow children to get their words or sounds out and to process what they mean so that they can explain it to us as the practitioner.

Sometimes a problem that is obvious to the children may be handled effectively in a different way. The teacher can say, 'You know, here's something that needs a longer discussion. Let's put it on our list of discussions we need to have.' Alternatively, getting back to the storytelling: 'This is an interesting problem, interesting story. Maybe someone would like to help me write it down so we can act it out. Put your name on the story list, and perhaps you can think of something in the story.' With experience, a teacher learns how to use this basic format to tease out ideas and help the drama go better. Because that is the common goal. Not to see how smart someone is, not to see how quickly someone can respond, but the play is the thing. The children understand and want to help improve the play once they realise that it is all a matter of how their story is constructed.

3 Build quality interactions with children. Show them right from the start that we have a genuine interest in them

The work of Vivian Gussin Paley states that we need to talk to each child in our care every day, and that we need to allow children to tell their stories by creating a classroom that is fair and inclusive through kindness and, I would add, listen effectively. How do we, as practitioners, ensure that every child is listened to and every child's voice is heard?

Practitioners need to show a genuine interest in the child and be involved in conversations from the start. Jools Page refers to this quality interaction as professional love and explains the importance of attachments with key persons as vital for communication and development (Clare, 2016).

4   Listen completely

'To truly listen to another is to give the other a voice. Hearing the voices of others is central to the pedagogy of listening' (Rinaldi, 2001).

Carla Rinaldi coined the phrase 'the pedagogy of listening' and focused on what is happening right now: 'listening not just with our ears, but with all of our senses (sight, touch, smell, taste, orientation)' (ibid.: 65). Piaget, Montessori and Golddshmied all place emphasis on the senses in our learning of language as a child. Listening needs time – time to be silent, to pause and to listen to ourselves.

We, as teachers and educators need to be listeners so we can inspire others to listen and be open to learning. Listening completely means practitioners need to be reflective. The ethos of a setting should provide opportunities for children to listen, but also talk and have time to make sense of their environment. Most language develops rapidly in the first few years of life, so many opportunities and experiences should be evident for children to support this development.

Practitioners need to reflect on the speech of the child in various ways. On different days, there are different ways of focusing and endless conversation, including between the teacher and her associates. Reflection at the end of the day may pose questions such as:

1   How did we achieve intimacy today?
2   What role did the teacher play?
3   Were we positive role models in our own speech and language?

5   Be positive role models when using language with children

Practitioners that work with children need to be positive in their attitude and energetic in their play with children. They need to be constantly reflecting on the best approaches for the unique child. They also need to ensure that they are not passive in their behaviour towards children and avoid the misconception that young children do not need as much opportunity for conversation. If anything, very young children need many opportunities to understand the rules of conversation. Be positive role models when using language with children.

The work of Bruner and Bandura suggests the role of the adult is essential for children to acquire language. Practitioners need to interact with children. They need to know which children need more time and longer interactions if they are not experiencing this interaction at home. Children need to hear correct pronunciation and know how sentences are structured in conversations through daily interaction with adults, from a very early age. Adults also need to tune in to the children in their care. They need to know the words that are meaningful to them and the how to interpret the sounds made.

6   Work in partnership with parents

Working with different family structures, so that they feel welcome and reassured, will ensure that children will settle.

In my experience, parents are the first to recognise that their children become more articulate and interesting when they make believe. Sharing information about the vocabulary that children use will help the practitioner use these words in the setting to observe if the child understands the vocabulary in context. Parents sharing the interests of the child with practitioners enables planning of the setting around those interests.

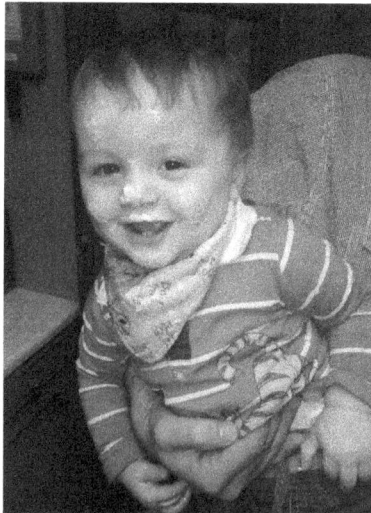

*Tactile play enables children to explore and think about how it feels,
what it smells and looks like or what they can hear*

7   Provide a sensory curriculum for the very young

Children need many opportunities to play with sensory materials such as clay, mud, sand and water. Tactile play enables children to explore and think about how it feels, what it smells and looks like or what they can hear. Vocabulary including words such as squeeze, soft, smooth, rustle, pop and light, bright or pale extends their descriptive language. Observing changes in materials supports children in their understanding of how and why things change and how to express these concepts.

8   Value a child's home language

Children who have English as an additional language are gaining an expertise in communication. They are learning to balance two languages and it is imperative that respect for the home language is demonstrated by the setting. A setting that makes time to learn familiar words the child may use at home demonstrates a positive environment where language is valued and respected.

If practitioners apply theory to practice, they are demonstrating that they are planning an enabling environment for children centred on play. Perceptions of play and learning ensure all children have the right to access a curriculum that is stimulating and motivating, within which they can flourish. Theories suggest that children need good quality interactions, positive role models and sensory play in the early years to find their voice and practitioners to nurture it. Legislation should promote the essential need for the voice of the child to be heard and practised in education. The voice of the child has never been more important in legislation.

The Childcare Act 2006 (DFE) was specifically for the early years. It set out the Early Years Foundation Stage (EYFS) curriculum into prime and specific areas (DFE, 2014b).

The prime areas are:

1   Communication and language (CL)
2   Personal social and emotional development (PSED)
3   Physical development (PD).

The specific areas are:

1   Literacy (L)
2   Maths (M)

3   Understanding the world (UTW)

4   Expressive art and design (EAD).

Two-year progress checks are essential for development

At two years old practitioners assess if children are developing in the prime areas. This is essential to identifying needs of those children that may need extra support in the prime areas of development.

Communication and language is emphasised as necessary before any formal literacy is introduced, which agrees, in principle, to the stages outlined by theorists. Children need as much experience as possible in communicating, talking and interacting before any formal communication is achieved.

Many initiatives have been put in place to support children who may have difficulties in their development and have been set up to improve the learning gap. The Early Years Pupil Premium (EYPP) is additional funding for early years settings to improve the education provided for disadvantaged three- and four-year-olds (DFE, 2014a).

How do we ensure that legislation is adhered to?

Policies and procedures of a setting encapsulate the law and regulatory bodies such as Ofsted make sure that the statutory requirements are followed, through the common inspection framework. This framework ensures that the voice of the child is evident in a setting, in decisions, making choices and in opportunities for play.

Response to legislation in the curriculum

Legislation is a positive step towards ensuring all children develop and learn in a positive enabling environment. However, often settings interpret legislation in a prescriptive way and pressures lead to the notion that all settings must follow the curriculum in a structured way. It should be remembered that the EYFS is guidance and can be adapted per the needs and interests of children in the setting.

> Inspection is primarily about evaluating how well individual children and learners benefit from the education provided by the school or provider. Inspection tests the school's or provider's response to individual needs by observing how well it helps all children and learners to make progress and fulfil their potential.
>
> Ofsted, 2015, section 14

Statutory requirements must be adhered to, but a setting needs to have a strong ethos and a clear, identifiable pedagogical approach, explaining why and how it ensures all children receive the best care and education in their setting.

More and more, it is becoming apparent that children need lots of opportunities for talk and for their voice to be heard in the setting; practitioners need to demonstrate how they are effective in listening to the voice of the child, not giving in to the pressure of inspections.

The voice of the child in the Early Year Foundation Stage curriculum 2014 (EYFS)

The EYFS has variations across the UK. For example, in Wales the area of language and communication is defined as 'language, literacy and communication'; in Scotland it is defined as 'languages'; and in Northern Ireland it is defined as 'language and literacy'. However, the aims are the same and in line with the legislation. The differences show that the individual needs of a region have been reflected on. For example, in Wales, emphasis is placed on the importance of the Welsh language as part of the identity of Welsh children to promote a sense of belonging. The English curriculum separates communication and language from literacy.

Prime areas are the focus from birth to three years old; specific areas are the focus from three to five years old. However, practitioners can lay good foundations for literacy from birth by giving young babies opportunities to foster a love of books by collecting a range of board books and tactile books and using finger play, rhymes and familiar songs from home to support the young baby's enjoyment (DFE, 2014b).

Summary of the chapter

Theoretical perspectives and philosophical approaches centred on the voice of the child include the Reggio Emilia approach and Forest schools, as well as the EYFS. Theorists believe that the role of the adult is essential if the voice of the child is to flourish and develop successfully. Legislation has ensured that the early years curriculum is deemed a priority in supporting children's early development and through the Childcare Act 2006, emphasising the prime areas that need fostering and planned opportunities for effective teaching and learning.

2 Understanding the stages of development

Listening to baby, birth to 12 months

Babies have a voice. This chapter will consider the importance of early speech and language and the value of listening, copying sounds, imitating and tuning in to the baby from birth. It will consider the developmental needs and stages of children from birth to one year old for speaking and listening, focusing on how children develop speech or other forms of communication. It will reflect on research into brain development and consider how early stimulation is essential and listening is imperative for development. It gives examples of how practitioners can support communication by forming positive relationships with parents and carers and listening to children at each stage of their development. It is crucial to emphasise that each child is unique and records of this uniqueness need to be apparent and displayed in the setting.

Children need to be listened to right from birth

In the previous chapter, theoretical approaches to speech and language considered the way that language is linked to thought and develops through exploration of all the senses from an early age. One of the many ways that children make sense of their environment is by listening and speaking. The practitioner needs to have a clear knowledge of development so that they can support emergent speech.

Babies have the mechanisms of speech and language well before they are born. During their time in the womb, researchers believe babies can hear sounds outside and that is why they can recognise familiar voices and patterns of language overheard before birth. Both nature and nurture influence development 'They intertwine in children's development' (David, 2004). All children have a voice. It is the responsibility of the practitioner to hear that voice by supporting and encouraging communication. A child's brain develops rapidly during the first five years of life, especially the first three years. It is a time of rapid growth in all the areas of learning such as personal, social, emotional, intellectual, physical and communication. The child's brain grows as she or he uses each of the senses: a neural connection develops within the brain. New experiences repeated many times help make these new connections, which shape the way the child thinks, behaves and learns, as well as the way a child feels. These new experiences are called synapses. New synapses between cells are constantly being formed, while others are broken or pruned away (Brotherson, 2009).

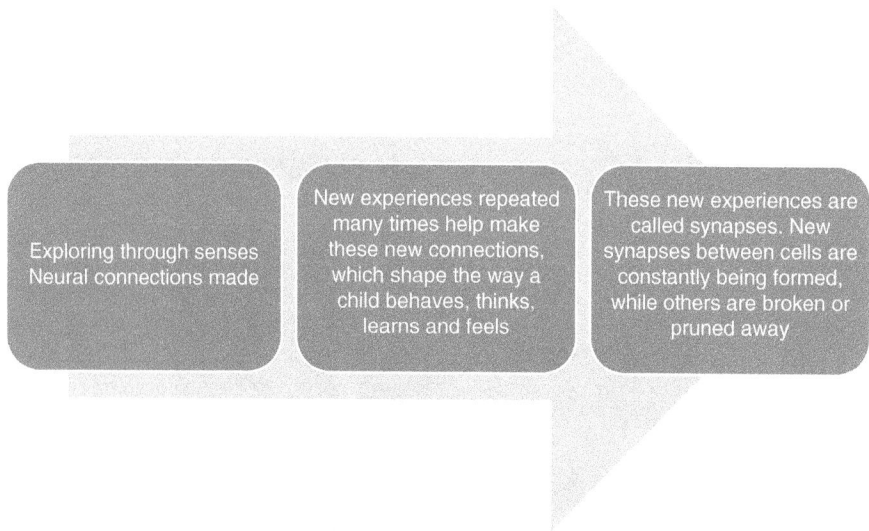

Exploring through senses Neural connections made

New experiences repeated many times help make these new connections, which shape the way a child behaves, thinks, learns and feels

These new experiences are called synapses. New synapses between cells are constantly being formed, while others are broken or pruned away

Figure 2.1 A baby's brain develops as she or he uses one of the senses

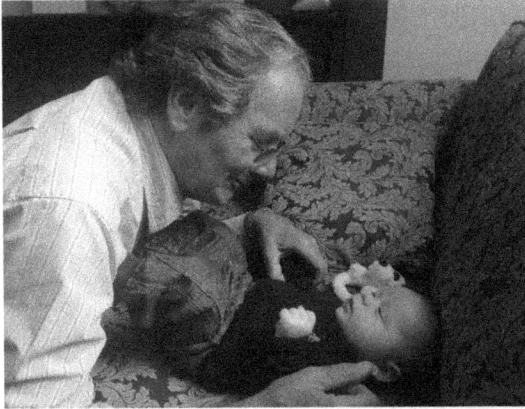

'The more loving and responsive the caregiver is, the greater the foundation for later social interaction'

The quality of experiences and relationships in the first three years of life has a deep and lasting impact on how the brain develops. The richer the environment, the greater the number of interconnections that are made. The larger the number of interconnections, the faster and more meaningful learning will be. By eight months of age a baby may have an astounding 1,000 trillion synapses in his brain. By late adolescence, about half of the 1,000 trillion synapses of the three-year-old will be discarded.

The emotional and physical environment in a baby's first few years needs to be full of love and care. The impact on the setting is that it needs to be stimulating and practitioners need to provide a secure and reassuring environment where babies can explore safely and begin to understand the world through using their senses.

The first year of life is critical for establishing trust, upon which all relationships are founded. 'The more loving and responsive the caregiver is, the greater the foundation for later social interaction' (Parent–Child Program, n.d.). Jools Page refers to it as 'professional love' (Page, 2015).

Lack of care, drug abuse and trauma can all have adverse effects on a child's social and emotional health. This has an impact on addressing issues such as poor parenting and how to give parents support and advice in the early years from birth as paramount to their development. Babies need positive interactions and communication right from the start. For children to develop in their speech and language, they need to form good attachments; by providing a positive environment, warm attachments are secured and enable a baby to want to communicate.

Many factors determine how effectively a child's speech progresses.

What language can a child speak?

The language that a child learns to speak depends on the language he or she has experience of in their early years. A child's brain adapts to a specific language that they hear and use. When a baby is three months old, his or her brain can distinguish several hundred different spoken sounds. Over the next several months, however, his or her brain will organise itself more efficiently so that it only recognises those spoken sounds that are part of the language that is regularly heard. During early childhood, the brain retains the ability to relearn sounds it has discarded, so young children typically learn new languages easily and without an accent. After about age ten, most children find it difficult to speak a foreign language as well as a native speaker if they only start to learn it then – even more so in adolescence or adulthood.

Do children learn language effectively from television?

Pantley (2013) suggested that mere exposure to language, such as listening to the television or to adults talking among themselves, provides little benefit. Experts suspect that babies younger than two years old view TV as a confusing array of colours, images and noises. They do not understand much of the content. Since the average TV scene lasts five to eight seconds, a baby or toddler does not have enough time to digest what is happening. Rather babies need to interact directly with other human beings, to hear people talking about what they are seeing and experiencing, for them to develop optimal language skills.

In a study on the transfer of learning between 2D and 3D sources during infancy, Barr (2013) wanted to discover what children would remember if they saw a two-dimensional (2D) demonstration (either by watching an action done first in a book, on a television or on a touchscreen) compared to a group who got no demonstration at all. She found that the children who got a (2D) demonstration did better than the control group, indicating that infants can learn from books, television and touchscreens.

However, the infants who saw a 2D demonstration imitated *50 per cent fewer actions* than infants that saw a live, three-dimensional (3D) demonstration. This indicates that it is a lot easier to learn from a live demonstration (ibid.). This is because it is difficult for children to understand how the symbols that they see in books and on screens transfer to the real, 3D world. Children will learn more from media when there are caring adults present who can support their learning.

Lisa Guernsey refers to as the '3 Cs': *content, context* and the individual *child* (Guernsey, 2012).

What are the main milestones in communication that underpin children's understanding of the world and themselves?

From birth to 12 months old, babies make sounds to express their needs, mainly by crying, initially, but also by nonverbal signals. Parents and practitioners who are close to the baby start to tune in to their voice.

Birth to three months old

- Reacts to loud sounds
- Calms down or smiles when spoken to
- Recognises your voice and calms down if crying
- When feeding, starts or stops sucking in response to sound
- Coos and makes pleasure sounds
- Has a special way of crying for different needs
- Smiles when he or she sees you

Four months old to six months old

- Smiles when he or she sees you
- Notices toys that make sounds

- Responds to changes in your voice
- Pays attention to music
- Babbles in a speech-like way and uses many different sounds, including sounds that begin with p, b and m
- Laughs

Seven months to one year old

- Imitates different speech sounds and has one or two words such as 'mama' or 'dada'
- Communicates using gestures such as waving or holding up arms
- Babbles using long and short groups of sounds ('tata', 'upup', 'bibibi')
- Responds to requests such as 'come here'
- Understands words for common items such as 'cup', 'chair', or 'shoe'

NIDCD, 2017

How do babies initially communicate and express their individuality?

Babies arrive in this world crying. Parents soon decipher the different needs for the different cries. Listening to a baby's cries is the first step in listening to their voice. They make sounds initially when they are born that are interpreted as: 'I need food', 'I want a cuddle', 'I am tired' or 'I want to play'.

Parents, practitioners and all adults involved in the baby's life need to tune in to these cries and not dismiss or ignore them, as this is the beginning of the voice of the child. It also has an impact on the staff employed to care and educate children. The most essential qualities that practitioners need is commitment and a genuine interest and love for children.

If the brain develops rapidly in the first three years of life and new synapses form quickly, contact with adults, whether it is the parent, extended family or practitioner must be warm and positive. The key person system plays a vital role as the practitioner needs to observe the baby, find out their likes and dislikes, talk to parents and extended family to discover their needs and how to support them in developing their voice.

Speaking is one component of language and language is linked to thought. It enables children from birth to know that the sounds that they make are given meaning. In addition, it helps them to make sense of their environment.

Language is vital to learning, so practitioners need to ask appropriate questions to extend children's learning and understanding of the world around them. The most essential factor is to develop a dialogue with children right from birth. It is important to listen to children and realise the importance of early speech and language, the value of listening, copying sounds and imitating; tuning into the baby in your care will support the baby's development in speaking skills.

Crying is a reflex and may have several meanings

- **C**uddles
- **R**umbling tummy
- **Y**ou just feel like it
- **I**llness
- **N**appy change
- **G**etting tired
- **T**emperature
- **I** just feel like crying
- **M**aking teeth
- **E**xcited or over excited

What are the good responses to a crying baby?

- **R**espond to the voice of the baby's cries
- **E**nable baby to feel relaxed by gentle rocking
- **S**uck on a comforter: dummy or not?
- **P**laying a soothing sound, the washing machine or the hoover
- **O**rganise time for a warm bath, massage or tummy rub
- **N**egotiate different positions
- **D**ecide on priorities

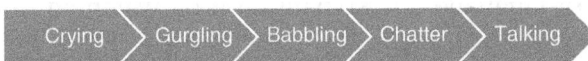

Crying > Gurgling > Babbling > Chatter > Talking

Figure 2.2 The journey of the voice: milestones from crying to gurgling to babbling to chatter to talking

Why are early experiences so important?

Early experiences can determine how proficient a child becomes in his or her language. Researchers found that when mothers frequently spoke to their children their vocabulary was more extensive than those peers whose mothers rarely spoke to them (Huttenlocher *et al.*, 1991; Hart and Risley, 1995). Moreover, speaking to baby begins even before a baby is born.

Babbling is an important milestone

Babies babble using the sounds they hear around them. The sounds, rhythm and tone in babble are influenced by the language the baby is exposed to. Repeated syllables such as 'da' or 'ba ba' are defined as *canonical babbling* (Iverson *et al.*, 2007). In an article by Tamekia Reece (2017), Sherry Artemenko, a speech-language pathologist and founder of Play on Words, suggests 'Babbling is an important milestone because it represents the beginning of real communication, when a baby starts experimenting with sounds, listening for a reaction, responding, and building social relationships' (Artemenko, cited in ibid.).

Once a baby has had practice using lips and tongue to form sounds, usually around six to seven months, babbles will become more speech-like. It may seem as though baby is just blurting out random sounds, but if you pay close attention, you will observe changes in tone and inflection when he or she talks. The voice may rise at the end of a string of babble, as though a baby is asking a question, or he or she may mumble under his or her breath after Aunt Ann goes overboard kissing both cheeks. You will also notice that a baby may pause after he or she says what is on his or her mind, seemingly waiting for a response. A baby learns that a conversation is a back-and-forth thing, not just one person going repeatedly.

The impact for practitioners is that babies need opportunities to sit and converse. Practitioners need to focus on what baby 'says' over how he says it. Tone, facial expressions and body language may demonstrate meaning. For example, a huge grin and bouncing up and down while he or she 'talks' probably means a baby is sharing exciting news. Chatter starts to form as a baby learns the rules of language and socialisation by watching how you react to sounds made.

The foundation stage curriculum provides opportunities for practitioners to foster a positive development of this speech.

Prime area: communication and language – speaking

Table 2.1 Birth to 11 months

A unique child	Positive relationships	Enabling environment
Communicates needs and feelings in a variety of ways such as gurgling, crying, babbling and squeaking	Work with parents to find out how they like to communicate, noting child's chosen language	Learn and use key words of baby's home language
Lifts hands in anticipation of being picked up	Ensure parents know the importance of talking in home language to baby	Provide recorders so that parents can record familiar comforting sounds such as lullabies
Gradually develops speech sounds to communicate with adults	Encourage baby sounds in turn-taking conversation	Use these to help babies to settle
Adults say 'baba', 'dada', 'no no'	Communicate with parents to update information on child's personal words	WhatsApp group

Birth to four months

Babies are born to listen. They will begin to associate sounds – for example, linking the family dog to a bark. Communication will be crying, but a baby will soon begin to use the tongue, lips and palate to make gurgles. Babies as young as four weeks can distinguish between similar syllables like 'ma' and 'nab'. As young as two months, they begin to associate certain sounds with certain lip movements; the rules of conversation are learnt very early on. Babies learn from 'the pleasurable response of key people' (Riddall-Leech, 2005: 86). When adults smile, they will respond with a smile or facial expression. They learn to wait and respond as they are finding their voice and are sociable with familiar adults communicating in a variety of ways with them.

Four to six months

Sighs give way to babbling. You will hear back-of-the-tongue sounds, such as *g* and *k*, and lip sounds *m, w, p* and *b*. In addition, the baby may recognise their name, but only as an important word, such as 'Hi!' or 'Bye!'. It is not until six months, at the earliest, that they will realise their name refers to themselves. They may not talk yet, but it turns out babies can recognise each other's emotions by five months of age, correctly matching the sounds of happy or frustrated infants with the appropriate facial expressions.

Seven to 12 months

Babbling will now begin to sound more like words. Sounds are repeated. At about nine months, gestures such as pointing and grunting indicate what a baby may want. The first word often appears around 12 months. Common first words may be greetings ('hi' or 'bye-bye'). Or they might be very concrete: people ('ma, ma' or 'da, da'), pets ('doggy' or 'kitty') or food ('cookie', 'juice' or 'milk'). A baby is slowly beginning to comprehend a few words – things like names and everyday objects such as 'bottle'.

Knowing the ages and stages of development, as a practitioner, enables the setting to plan appropriate and stimulating activities around routines to ensure babies are progressing in their speech. Early years settings need to provide opportunities for babies to achieve their milestones and have observation methods in place that identify babies that are not achieving their milestones. It is vital that practitioners and parents work together. Effective communication needs practitioners to carefully listen to babies and know when and how to respond. This is a real skill; it is important not to jump in too quickly or be too slow in our responses with babies. It is also important not to wait for the child to make sounds to respond. They may show they are interacting in other ways such as gesturing or facial expression, so it is important to respond to these visual signs as well.

Checklist of good practice

1 Value key words used at home

Home language should be valued. A good practice setting would carry out a home visit where the key person knows the familiar words used with the baby at home and can transfer it into the setting. These words may be words for family members, may be in the home language or may be words used by the family. Family names, including the name of pets, should be recorded and may be used in the setting with the baby. Communicate with parents to update information on a child's personal words. Ensure parents know the importance of talking in the home language to baby.

2 Find out sleep routine

Good practice could also ask parents to record how they get their children to sleep. Do they have a favourite lullaby, are they rocked to sleep, do they have the lights out and music on?

This all helps to reassure the baby, keeping routines similar so that the baby feels secure. In addition, if a baby has a comforter, they may cry out for it during naptime.

3 Use social networks to have opportunities to listen to baby

WhatsApp groups, Facebook pages and FaceTime all help practitioners listen to the baby in their own home and help them, further, to tune in to the baby and vice versa.

Remember, confidentiality and safeguarding rules need to apply.

4 Encourage home observations

Ask parents to jot down the sounds that baby makes and encourage baby sounds in turn-taking conversation. Keep up to date with the information when new sounds are made and when sounds related to specific things are discovered. Share information with each other, observing the children's responses and recording this in their record. What interests them, what do they like?

We need to respect children to accommodate their voice.

5 Provide parents with opportunities to extend vocabulary and explore using senses

Engaging in conversations with babies may speed up their language development more than simply talking at them or around them. Allow babies to be part of conversations.

6 Share your observations regularly with parents

Encourage them to share their observations with you. Babies may be attempting to say words said by familiar adults in their lives and babble their name, which makes sense to them, but may be ignored or missed as an opportunity by the practitioner if they haven't spoken and discussed the child's language with parents.

Observations allow the practitioner and parent to see the child's view of the world. Using treasure baskets with resources that make a noise can improve children's listening skills from an early age. The link between language and thought is crucial and children need time to gather their thoughts and to verbalise when problem-solving to make sense of their environment.

7 Understand that two-way communication begins from birth

Interaction is essential. Babies respond to faces and respond to facial expressions. Communication is linked to social development and babies need many opportunities for interactive activities to develop in their language. This interaction also enables them to make sense of the world and develops their cognition. Games such as 'peek a boo' allow the baby to anticipate, respond and look for a reaction, which is the beginning of communication.

Babbling requires a response. Babies babble in a speech-like way and use many different sounds, including sounds that begin with p, b and m. Babbling usually refers to an object that the baby is drawn to. He or she is giving meaning to something they see, hold, hear or taste. Babbling is also a baby's response to experiences shared with parents and practitioners: a response to their understanding. This is when they begin to imitate different speech sounds and have one or two words, such as 'mama' or 'dada'.

8 Provide a range of language

Children need to hear plenty of language and in a variety of ways. Songs, actions signing and gestures all provide babies with opportunities to make sense of the world of conversation.

9 Quality interactions: familiar faces and calm voices

Making time for your key children ensures that babies, from an early age, receive quality interactions. Examples include sharing a story or singing together. Practitioners need to just sit with the baby in their care and talk, repeating sounds and forming secure attachments. Musical toys or even looking in a mirror with a baby are activities that will engage a baby from an early age. By repeating familiar words in the routines of the day, babies will become accustomed to the sound of these familiar words and the meaning.

10 Laughter: make them laugh and laugh with them

Have fun with the baby in your care. Finding out what makes a baby laugh and interact will ensure that secure attachments are made and the voice of the child fostered. Listening to laughter and giggles of a baby is one of the most beautiful sounds to the human ear and one which ensures the adult remains and continues to play and interact.

Case study

Thomas has a close relationship with both sets of grandparents, Grandpa and Grandma live close by and he is lucky enough to be able to see them every week, when he is taken out to lots of exciting places! When Mummy and Daddy arrive to pick Thomas up from Grandma and Grandpa's house, he is very enthusiastic to tell Mummy and Daddy all that he has seen and done that day.

From observing Thomas with family and friends, since birth, it is apparent that speech development is flourishing and Thomas is completely part of conversations and communication, and has been since he was a baby.

When Thomas was six months, his grandad started communicating by using a finger up and down on his lips, making a blubber sound. Grandad explains:

'I used this as a kind of bonding as it was our own little signal. I did it recently and he remembered it and gave a lovely smile. It was before he could communicate, so was a personal gesture as no one else used it.'

Grandad also made a point of acknowledging his long gurgling efforts as if they were language through facial expressions, affirming language and head movement.

(continued)

Speaking to Thomas as a baby

Both parents interacted very well with Thomas from birth. They made eye contact, had warm positive interactions made good attachments from birth, so that Thomas felt part of a family. They repeated sounds, using lots of animation and gestures in their communication.

They waited for a response or acknowledgement from Thomas when they asked him questions from a very early age. For example, getting him dressed, Mum or Dad would say, 'Shall we get your shoes on? Where are your trousers?' He would look at them and smile or gurgle before the conversation continued.

Music was a strong focus for Thomas and, from a very young age, he joined a music group where the parents and babies joined in with nursery rhymes and songs repeated weekly.

'Parentese' helps young children pick out words from sentences

'Parentese' refers to the exaggerated speech caregivers tend to use with babies. It involves lots of repetition, animation in the voice, longer speech sounds and a slower pace (Lowry, 2013).

Gestures enable babies to focus on something that grabs their attention. Routines for Thomas involved many gestures for him to understand when it was bedtime or bath time. Thomas knew from a young age that when parents lifted their arms it meant 'up'; Thomas would copy this action, eventually followed by a sound and then a word. Gestures support children in developing much stronger language skills from an early age. They also put their hands to their mouths when something was hot (as well as saying hot), so he understood not to touch hot things/to stay away from heat.

Introducing interesting vocabulary from a young age

Thomas's parents spoke to Thomas in full sentences a great deal of the time, emphasising key words with actions. For example, they would say: 'We are going to see Uncle OLLIE today and Uncle ADAM and we can all go to the PARK as it's so SUNNY.' Familiar people to Thomas became easy to understand when their names were emphasised in a sentence. Words that explained what was happening were also emphasised and repeated

(continued)

when they arrived at the park. Trips to the seaside involved words that Thomas could feel. A windy day, cold, shivering, hot, paddling – all quickly became part of the vocabulary that he could use in different environments as he could feel the word (Zauche et al., 2016). Zauche and her colleagues from Atlanta, Georgia, set out to determine which factors had the biggest impact on children's language development. They looked at 103 studies of children's language outcomes to figure out the key ingredients of language nutrition. The amount of speech directed towards children has a very important influence on their vocabulary; however, it's not just about how many words children hear. The researchers also found that children need to hear words within motivating, back-and-forth conversations to learn (ibid.).

Thomas has an extensive vocabulary with words that motivate him. From an early age, Thomas travelled on local transport as parents worked in the city and visited relatives around the country and in different countries. As Mum prepared for a journey, she would talk to Thomas about the train, tube, DLR or bus; again, emphasising these words gave Thomas an understanding of the different modes of transport. Grandpa explains things to Thomas in great detail and as a result Thomas is able to explain how "enormous" the engines are that he has seen at the Bluebell railway, for example. He has often learnt lots of new words having spent a day with Grandma and Grandpa.

Even the word aeroplane enthused Thomas with excitement and anticipation as he began to realise this meant visiting his grandad and nanny in Ireland. Thomas was part of conversations right from the beginning, which led him to anticipate things and recognise familiar names.

Reflective questions for the student

Reflect on your own role in relation to the provision for supporting speech, language and communication development in the setting.

Can you identify gestures that you use in the setting with children in your care?

Do babies and children respond with their own gestures?

How can you create a language-rich environment in the setting to extend a child's language?

What activites can support the development of speech, language and communication of children aged:

- 0–1 year 11 months
- 2–2 years 11 months
- 3–5 years?

Summary of the chapter

From birth babies have a voice. Crying, gurgling and babbling are examples of how babies begin their interactions with adults. They need quality interactions to develop their voice. Early experiences are vital for this. It is important to understand that communication is a two-way process from birth and that partnership with parents is vital for the voice of the child. Including parents in the setting by valuing their home language, including them in observations, finding out sleep routines and using social media as a positive tool ensures both practitioners and parents work together to support the voice of the baby at a crucial time. Placing emphasis on the importance of early speech sounds requires everyone who cares for the baby to respond and interact with these sounds in a positive, fun way.

3 | Development from 12 months to three years

From 12 months to three years, children are energetic in their movements and in their language acquisition. Some of the key areas of development are two-word combinations and using verbs in their conversation. As babies approach two years old, they are inquisitive and curious. They want to find out how things work; they are learning to share and take turns, negotiate and have words for almost everything. Observing children will support the practitioner in deciphering their needs and interests, which can extend their vocabulary. Observing and interacting with children will enable the

(continued)

practitioner to communicate with the children in their care, 'tuning into' their speech. Tassoni (2014) argued that the length of interaction is critical for children and those with the greatest need should have the greatest time. There is a need to target specific children on their learning journey. By the end of two years old, the progress check should indicate:

- what skills, experiences and knowledge we expect children to have;
- what opportunities these children are receiving at home;
- what are they not getting at home and how can practitioners plan for this?

Quality interaction needs CARE

- Connect
- Adults
- Routines
- Engage

CARE

Connect: practitioners need to enjoy being with the children in their care. They need to demonstrate they are enjoying the time spent with the children. Being connected motivates children to stay in the interaction longer and, therefore, provides them with more opportunities to learn.

Adults: conversations that provide the best context for a child to build their language and literacy skills are those in which adults play an interactive part in the conversation by: enjoying the company of each other; following the child's lead; talking about what interests him and the adult; and keeping the conversation going, if possible.

Routines: routines are repetitive, the words and actions used in the routine become predictable, making it easier for children to learn them. Routines also indicate how much the voice of the child has been listened to. The very start of the day is a time practitioners should not dismiss or hurry. It indicates the mood the child may be in and how they feel about being there. Nothing might be said, but their voice is still apparent in the way that they feel. Practitioners need to consider, from the child's perspective, how they feel: are they glad to be there and do they feel as if they belong? Routines can demonstrate to a child that they do belong. The practitioner may have listened to the voice of the child and picked up familiar words that the child uses at snack time, toileting or nap time. A good setting involves parents in routines, finding out sleeping routines at home and using favourite music or allowing comfort objects that ensure the child feels secure and cared for. If a child feels that they belong and have a sense of identity, they know that the practitioners will listen and take notice and that their voice will be heard loud and clear. If a child is distressed, the key person needs to find out why.

Engage: for successful quality interaction, practitioners need to join in and engage with play and the child will pay attention to what the adult is saying and doing. For example, during role play in the setting, practitioners may have set up the area as a hospital. The vocabulary surrounding the hospital – what it is used for, thermometers, needles – will extend a child's vocabulary, understanding and imagination. Practitioners need to enhance this play.

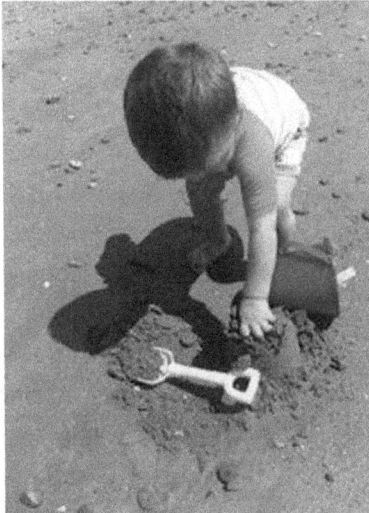

Physical development and language acquisition

From 12 months, babies are beginning to walk, run and starting to climb. They become more inquisitive as their world widens, giving them opportunities to learn names for their movement and increasing their vocabulary as they encounter new experiences. Physical development quickens at this stage with movement and managing risks develops confidence in babies. Physical skills are largely linked to language as babies reach out to ask for help as they are climbing, or cry if they fall. They want to explore and discover new corners of the setting or home that lead to more discoveries and more vocabulary. Froebel (Bruce, 2012) valued play and choice in learning; he considered the outdoor environment essential. Walks, space and light were important to growth and development. Added to this was the value of sounds produced by different materials. Listening opportunities outdoors give rise to questions, curiosity and enjoyment in copying or mimicking sounds. The sound of the birds, the sound of people, transport or the wind. Babies start to take it all in as they are out and about with the family. Life is on the move for baby as they begin walking. Many experiences or opportunities for speech can be linked to physical development. The physical attributes of speech, learning how to move the tongue to produce certain sounds, are now essential for development.

What is meant by two-word combinations?

Children begin to say their first words around 15 months and start to combine words at around 24 months, including verbs in their vocabulary (Hagan *et al.*, 2008). This rapid development needs constant monitoring as children can start to fall back in their development if there are not quality interactions and age-appropriate resources evident. Practitioners need to have a clear understanding of speech development, particularly in the early years; they need to use gestures with words.

A study by Rudolph and Leonard (2016) in early language milestones examined combinations, and whether delays in these milestones predicted later language problems. Interestingly, children who were late to combine words were more at risk of future problems with language than children who were late with their first word. Many children may say 'night' or 'bye bye'. In effect, these are not two-word combinations. True two-word combinations express two separate ideas. For example, Mummy go or me bottle. Using several single words is an indicator that a child may be ready to combine words. They may often use a word and a gesture; this is an opportunity for practitioners to interpret the gesture. For example, a child may say me and point to the banana. This is an indicator that the child in your care is ready for two-word combinations, but I would continue to use gestures with the words.

For this reason, the two-year progress check is vital as it identifies whether there may be a speech delay.

Including verbs in conversations

Children will add verbs to their vocabulary that are meaningful to them and that is why the outdoors provides opportunities for children to widen their vocabulary through experiences. Examples of verbs used initially are:

bite, blow, break, bring, bump, clean, close, cry, dance, draw, drink, drive, eat, fall, feed, finish, get, give, go, help, hit, hug, hurry, jump, kick, kiss, look, love, open, play, pull, push, put, read, ride, run, say, see, show, sing, sleep, smile, splash, stop, swim, swing, take, throw, tickle, touch, walk, wash, watch, wipe, write.

Fenson *et al.*, 2007

A recent study showed that two-year-old children who use more verbs have more advanced grammatical skills six months later. Introducing verbs may begin with a few and increase so that by 40 months a child should be using up to 40 verbs (Hadley *et al.*, 2016).

Ages and stages of development

12 months to three years

12–18 months

During this time, first words usually appear (these one-word utterances are rich with meaning). In the following months, babies continue to add more words to their vocabulary. Babies can understand more than they say, though, and will be able to follow simple instructions. In fact, a baby can understand you when you say 'No' – although they will not always obey!

18 months to two years: baby to toddler

In their second year, a toddler's vocabulary has grown and they will start to put two words together into short 'sentences'. They will understand much of what is said to them, and you will be able to understand what they say to you (most of the time!).

Two to three years

At this age, a child will be able to speak in longer, more complex sentences and use a greater variety of speech sounds more accurately when they speaks. They might play and talk at the same time. Strangers will probably be able to understand most of what is said by the time a child is three.

Milestones

Milestones include:

- building up vocabulary that extends their world such as knowing a few parts of the body and being able to point to them when asked. Repeating rhymes such as 'Head, shoulders, knees and toes' will enable children to remember their body parts in a fun way;

- starting to acquire new words on a regular basis. Enjoying familiar stories with a child can enable them to remember key words or phrases that can then be included into their conversations. It will give them the opportunity to point to pictures, when named, in books. This will help children to extend their vocabulary and use words for meaning;

- following simple commands and understanding simple questions. This can be achieved through gestures and pictures;

- using some one- or two-word questions and putting two words together. Practitioners need to repeat one-word utterances with two words or a sentence. Using familiar phrases can also support children with two- or three-word utterances;

- using many different consonant sounds at the beginning of words. By using sounds in play and exaggerating the beginning consonant, the child may be supported in understanding consonants.

NIDCD, 2017

Prime area: communication and language

Table 3.1 12–16 months

Unique child	Positive relationships	Enabling environment
Uses sounds in play: brrrm, car	Tune in to the baby When babies try to say a word, repeat it back	Find out words that the children use that are important to them
Uses single words		Explain that the strong
Imitates words and sounds	Find out from parents	foundations in a
Eye gaze to make requests	about greetings used in home language	home language support the
Creates personal words	Value all language spoken	development of English

Source: DFE, 2014b

Table 3.2 16–26 months

Unique child	Positive relationships	Enabling environment
Use familiar expressions, e.g. 'Oh dear, all gone'	Give choices, e.g. apple or banana	Allow time to follow children's lead and
Use different types of everyday words, such as 'banana', 'walk', 'go', 'hot'	Model building sentences Child says 'car' Adult says 'mummy's car' Show children how to	have fun together while developing language
Begin to ask simple questions	pronounce or use words by repeating in the	Plan to talk through some activities Provide stories with
Begin to talk about people that are not present	correct way Support children using a variety of strategies, e.g. signing	repetitive phrases

Source: DFE, 2014b

12–16 months

Babies are now becoming more sociable as their world opens up. They start to look to where a sound is coming from. For example, if an adult is on the other side of the room and calls their name they will turn towards the sound. They will notice sounds and decipher familiar and unfamiliar sounds, sometimes getting scared of unknown sounds. Babies also begin to understand familiar words that are used a lot and often used with gestures such as no or look or hello. They can follow simple instructions and use gestures to communicate by pointing or looking at objects they want. They start to gain attention by using sounds, gestures or pointing to express their needs.

16–20 months

At this stage of development, babies are beginning to choose and show their preferences. 'Allowing babies to make choices encourages them to negotiate, cooperate and problem solve' (Riddall-Leech, 2005: 90). Making choices also needs to address when conflict arises and how to resolve it.

Babble begins to turn into sounds and then words, such as night, bye bye. They love interactive games such as 'peek a boo' and will let the adult know through gestures sounds or words, such as again again, that they want to play more. They enjoy conversations and will babble and make sounds or even simple words in response to you.

By two years old

By this age, children generally:

- concentrate on activities for longer, like playing with a toy;
- sit and listen to simple stories with pictures;
- understand between 200 and 500 words;
- understand more simple questions and instructions – for example, 'Where is your shoe?' and 'Show me your nose';
- copy sounds and words a lot;
- use 50 or more single words. These will also become more recognisable to others;
- start to put short sentences together with two to three words, such as 'more juice' or 'bye nanny';
- enjoy pretend play with their toys, such as feeding dolly;
- use a limited number of sounds in their words – often these are p, b, t, d, m and w. Children will also often miss the ends off words at this stage. They can usually be understood about half of the time.

NIDCD, 2017

At this stage of their development children need opportunities for speech and they need adult support to extend and enhance their learning. 'If children articulate their thinking, their parents, teachers and other educators are in a better position to help them refine and further develop their ideas' (Nutbrown, 1994: 5). This stage of development is essential, as it is the beginning of articulation.

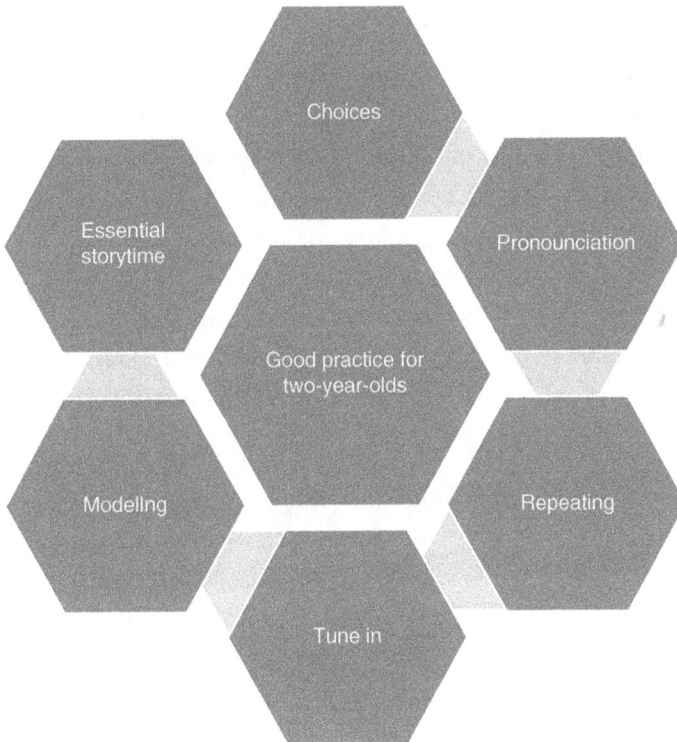

Figure 3.1 Good practice for two-year-olds

Checklist of good practice

Emphasise a variety of words

Model short, grammatical sentences. Even though children's first word combinations lack proper *structure*, add *gestures to your words* and *model correct sentences*.

In terms of grammar (e.g. 'go car', 'want juice', 'me up'), it is important that you provide your child with models that are grammatically correct. This helps your child understand the meaning and structure of words. For example, if your child says 'go car' when he is getting in the car, you can say 'You are going in the car.' Alternatively, if your child says 'want juice', you could say 'Do you want some juice?'

Babies may vocalise in two- or three-word phrases. Extending this to sentences enables babies to see how words fit together.

Give opportunities for choices

Babies start to use gestures to communicate by pointing or looking at an object they want. This is an opportunity for practitioners and adults caring for babies to give a name and meaning to the object they may point to it. It is an opportunity to pick up different objects to see if they choose the one they were pointing to with their finger. Using the vocabulary for the object gives it a meaning and repeating the word allows the baby to be familiar with this word.

Between 16 months to two years old, babies can start to develop an understanding of choice. With choice comes language, vocabulary, signs and gestures that enable them to interact, demonstrating their understanding but also their preferences.

Babies may make choices about what colour t-shirt they want to wear by pointing to the t-shirt or what toy they want to play with.

Meaningful words enable the baby to make choices and to increase their vocabulary.

Saying no

Sometimes a baby may choose to do something that is not permitted, so practitioners are sowing the seed at this age for babies to understand 'no' and why something may not be allowed, enabling them to learn the skills of how to negotiate, compromise or resolve conflict. As they move around the plug socket becomes an interesting thing to explore, as do the oven or fridge doors that open or close in the home. In the setting, risk assessments should ensure that children are safe, but also understand the importance of not touching plug sockets.

Pronunciation

It is important to be clear when using words with children and to say the word with clarity. Pronunciation needs to respect accents and value different dialects.

We do not all say words in the same static way, but we do pronounce the words so that we are understood. Babies need to hear the correct pronunciation for them to develop it correctly in their speech.

Hearing words repeated back to them

There are a variety of ways that babies can hear words repeated back to them. At the end of the day, when parents arrive to collect their child, practitioners can repeat the phrase or words used, recalling the event with parents.

Adults that tune in to their talk

Knowing children's favourite phrases or words will help practitioners find out their interests. Knowing the names of familiar family and friends in a child's life will enable a practitioner to converse and interact with a child about things that are meaningful to them. Stories may start with conversations, talking to children about what they like or what they are doing. Gestures and actions may form part of stories that can extend children's imagination.

Many opportunities for stories

Vivien Gussin Paley explains that we need to listen to children's stories; practitioners need to make the role play area much more extensive and accessible to very young children so that they can retell stories through imaginative play or make up their own stories. Many children enjoy superhero play, which practitioners often find irritating and believe gets out of control. However, a child's choice is their voice and needs to be channelled into a positive experience. Practitioners need to interpret children's play even when the voice is silent.

Practitioners are constantly learning new ways of responding to the voice of the child and reflecting on practice. Vivien Gussin Paley describes some energetic superhero play as serious drama and explains it as play that the practitioner needs to make sense of as it is a style that belongs to the child. 'If I have not yet learned to love Darth Vader, I have at least made some useful discoveries while watching him play' (Gussin Paley, 1990).

Two-year progress check

In the first chapter, I reflected on the two-year progress check to identify children who were not reaching their milestones. It can inform a practitioner, parent or health visitor on the next steps to successful learning.

Table 3.3 Example of format for two-year progress check

Prime areas	Key person comments	Parents comments	Health visitor comments	Next steps to support learning and development
This would include a summary of the prime areas of development and record such things as two-word combinations, using verbs	The key person would comment here on what opportunities children receive at the setting or settings and how it impacts on practice	Parents would be asked to share opportunities that these children are receiving at home and what are they not getting at home; practitioners need to plan for this	Can the health visitor suggest support groups or where parents can get further advice?	Next steps should be given a time span and show how parents and the setting can support the child to be successful in their next steps When will we meet again?

The two-year progress check is a statutory requirement for all early years settings. Childminders, pre-schools and private nurseries all need to record a summary of a child's development and progress and identify next steps.

A summary of the prime areas of learning is recorded and both the setting and health visitor should see parent to discuss the child's development. It is an opportunity to flag up any factors that may be hindering progress and decide on how to assess, observe and support the child in achieving the milestones.

The two-year progress check can also be an opportunity to record words and phrases that the child is using and give advice on how to support the child in his or her progression of language. A check explains to parents how they can support their child in his or her voice.

The progress check can be the baseline from which to form an accurate picture of where the child is in the prime areas of learning, evaluating their progress and suggesting how they can progress.

Identifying needs that may affect development

The two-year progress check might determine factors that may influence development and enable the practitioner, with parents, to obtain the necessary help and support. However, it is important to remember that children develop at different rates and may pass through the stages quickly or slowly or might have a specific condition that may impinge on their development. Early intervention is crucial; thus, understanding general stages of development is important in helping practitioners to identify specific needs.

An example of the importance of early intervention: reflection from Carole Spraget, early years consultant and owner of Buxton Bears pre-school

Early identification of any issues in a child's development is critical for their future progress. Early intervention means a child and their family can seek the support and advice they need.

Often parents are unaware that their child has any developmental delay (especially, if it is their first child), so approaching parents must be done carefully and in a way that the parent does not feel that they or their child has 'done something wrong'. Handled carefully, parents are usually willing to accept support, advice and are also willing for us to refer their child on to a specialist such as a 'speech therapist' or an 'educational psychologist'. We have had two children this year that we have referred because of poor language development, both of whom are now receiving speech therapy sessions on a one-to-one basis; both now have a support plan in place in our own setting.

Many parents will admit that they thought there may have been a problem themselves, but were scared to voice their concerns (various reasons are given at this point, which often include the fear of their child being treated differently or that their child would not be accepted by their peers). This was the case a few years ago, with a mother whose child was eventually diagnosed as autistic.

Sadly, as in a case I was involved with this year, the parent felt that her child would be treated differently and she expressed her concerns that social services would be involved, but mainly it was that she felt by signing referral forms she was, in fact, giving up on her child! After spending some considerable time with both parents, trying to reassure them that they had nothing to fear and that it was in their child's best interest for an assessment referral to go ahead, they would only admit their child was 'difficult'; they still refused to sign the forms and, unfortunately, removed their child from our setting! In my professional opinion, the child had severe developmental delay which included language, behaviour and understanding.

Identifying when a child has additional needs may be easy when the child displays poor language abilities or strong visible behaviour difficulties and intervention can take place within a short time of starting at a pre-school setting such as ours. But sometimes it's not so evident and staff have to use observations, monitoring individual progress and their own knowledge of the child to identify if the child isn't making steady age-appropriate progress and by building up evidence in this way. Although it is a slower process, it does give a clearer view to any potential outside professional of where the child is and of the child's learning journey that has taken place so far, thus supporting their ability to offer the right help and advice as quickly as possible.

Quite often, a child that has gained extra support in the early years makes good progress and that support is often not needed by the time the child is ready to transfer into mainstream school, especially in the case of speech delay. But when no intervention has taken place the child is more likely to suffer the consequences later in their school life, when the gap between them and their peers deepens; this can lead not only to the child feeling low self-esteem, but also in them still requiring the support that could have been given much earlier in their development.

Ages and stages of development

Two to three years old

Babies are now known as toddlers. They are inquisitive and curious, they want to find out and know how things work; they are learning to share and take turns, negotiate and have words for almost everything. Some of these words may be instantly recognisable by families and practitioners. Toddlers start to use two- or three-word phrases.

Milestones

Milestones include:

- names objects to ask for them or to direct attention to them;
- speaks in a way that is understood by family members and friends;
- uses k, g, f, t, d and n sounds;
- uses two- or three-word phrases to talk about and ask for things;
- has a word for almost everything.

Table 3.4 Two to three years old

Unique child	Positive relationships	Enabling environment
Holds a conversation jumping from topic to topic	Wait and allow the child time to start conversations	Display objects and photos to show familiar events
Learns new words	Follow the child's lead	Provide activities which help children distinguish sounds and word patterns
Uses gestures	Give children thinking time	
Uses a variety of questions		
Uses simple sentences such as 'mummy gone work'	For English as an additional language (EAL) children value nonverbal communication and that offered in home language	Plan activities stories that have repetitive phrases
Beginning to use word endings		Help children build up vocabulary by extending the range of their experiences
	Add words to what children say	

Remember: children are different and develop skills at different times.

Checklist of good practice

1   Conversations are essential; use objects or experiences to talk to the child and wait for a response. Allow children to lead conversations.

2   Organise the enabling environment; include the children in planning, give them choices and take in to account their interests.

3   Never ignore a child. As practitioners our lives are busy, but the most important person in the room is the child, so it is imperative that we do not talk over children or ignore them, but ensure they feel valued and listened to.

4   Value children in your care; find out their interests, the words they use for routines, their family members and places that they go. Encourage them to join in conversations.

5   Endings of words: emphasise ending of words to support the understanding of the past present or future.

6   Repeat back words with good pronunciation rhyme time. Ask questions and respond to questions.

7   Share good practice. Work in partnership with parents and have conversations with parents.

8   Engage in conversations as much as possible.

Case study

Thomas, two to three years old

Today, at two years and six months old, I meet Thomas at Canary Wharf with his mum. He knows my daughter and I will be there as his mum has told him this and he has internalised this in his brain.

As he sees us, he runs towards us and gives us a big cuddle. He tells us about the train, the Docklands Light Railway (DLR) that he has arrived on and points at a DLR train as it passes by.

He talks about the train having no driver, but says he was the driver because he sat at the front of the train. Mum explains that she has started to talk about the mechanism of the train and this led to lots of questioning. Thomas is now extending further his vocabulary and digesting the new information and will continue to digest this information until he understands it and can retain it and then share it with others.

Thomas talks about going on an aeroplane to see Nan and Grandad and tells me a story that Grandad told him on FaceTime

His interests around transport enthuse his parents to visit the local steam train at Ridgeway Park in Chingford.

FaceTime

Technology can be an enormous advantage to learning language, but only if there is interaction. Overheard speech or language from media viewing does not promote children's language skills – for example, when they hear language though various media (like watching TV or viewing something on a computer or iPad).

However, when technology is used as a tool to enhance interaction, it can be very successful. Thomas would often bring the iPad to us when he was younger and say 'Nana'; he was always so excited to see those he knew on the screen.

Grandad told Thomas about the tractor in his garden. He went into intricate detail about the tractor digging and moving through the garden.

(continued)

53

Thomas retells the story to me and uses interesting vocabulary, explaining the movement of the tractor.

Toys and resources have supported Thomas's love of transport and his dad explains that one of his favourite toys is the excavator (which Thomas pronounces as inoculator). He has explained this to Thomas and Thomas now uses this word when he wants his toy.

When we drove to Hastings recently we saw a building site and his dad pointed out all the machines – including the excavator. Thomas was *so* excited to see the building site; when he was a good boy the following week Daddy bought him the excavator that they saw in the toy shop.

All children have an innate sense to develop speech and language as described by Chomsky using the term 'LAD' (language acquisition device). They store learnt information by means of the system Bruner described as LASS (language acquisition support system), which needs adults to interact with a child from birth, include them in conversations, introduce exciting vocabulary around the interests of the child and provide a language-rich environment.

The extent to which both parents played with Thomas, engaging him in learning activities and teaching him about new things, was associated with improved language and cognitive skills. As Thomas approaches three, he is very articulate; when putting his side of an argument forward he can success-fully reason things to others – explaining why he doesn't want to do some-thing – it may be 'boring' or he 'will do it later'.

He can tell us what he is feeling – whether he is unwell or happy (which he does say to us) – and he can tell us how he feels about others. 'I just love Ciara so much' or 'Someone at nursery is naughty, Mummy, and she did push me today.'

We believe that his speech has also helped enormously with his toilet training as he can tell us when he needs to go! He also understands that sometimes he must wait (for example, if we are driving) until he gets home, which he can do. Meal times are also a special part of family life – we are a close family unit and often go for Sunday lunch with Grandma, Grandpa, Uncle Ollie and Uncle Adam. Thomas loves to join in with the conversa-tion and be part of the questions asked and as he is growing up he is par-ticipating in asking more of the questions too which is great. Routines such as meal times need to be full of conversations and enjoyed.

Reflective questions for the student

Reflect on your own role in relation to the provision of supporting speech, language and communication development in own setting.

How can the use of technology support the development of speech, language and communication?

Can you explain the benefits of holistic development when supporting speech, language and communication development?

How do you include the child's interests in a language-rich environment?

Summary of the chapter

From 12 months to three years, children are energetic. There is a link between movement and increased vocabulary as the actions that children do have words attached. For example, they run fast, they climb up to the top, they jump and splash in puddles. Observing and interacting with children will enable the practitioner to communicate with the children in their care, 'tuning into' their speech. The good length and quality of inter-action is essential for children and those with the greatest need should have the greatest time. There is a need to target specific children on their learning journey. Early intervention is vital at this stage for children that need support in achieving the milestones in this age bracket. Conversa-tions enable children to build up their vocabulary and their voice needs to be heard.

School readiness

Speech and language development for three to five years

4

At three years, children are inquisitive about the word around them, asking questions and trying to work things out. They are beginning to share and take turns, playing together and become independent in their learning. This is the time for meaningful conversations and ample opportunities should be available for children to be included that provide opportunities to build language and literacy skills. Children's language is full of vocabulary and phrases that help them to negotiate, resolve conflicts, form friendships, make choices and learn to share and compromise.

Children listen to a story and are given opportunities to talk about the story

School readiness involves talking in longer, complex sentences and practition-ers need to prepare children for this way of speaking and understanding. School readiness is about learning to read and write, but, as seen in the case study of Thomas, activities provided in earlier years lay the foundations for reading and writing well before school readiness. Before the age of three years old, young children are already pointing out words in print that they see. Most chil-dren know the signs for local shops or favourite restaurants or point out printed words on the cereal box. They start making marks from a very early age in all sorts of sensory contexts as they squeeze, pull and push materials such as Play-Doh to build up their fine motor muscles. As they develop, they use pencils, pens and brushes to form marks they interpret as words or letters and may write pretend shopping lists, telephone numbers or stories. Young children learn best about literacy by talking and interacting with practitioners and parents about the things that interest them in their daily life. School readiness arguably starts at three years old as, by four years old, many children will start formal schooling and be a member of the reception class. School readiness is highlighted in the EYFS curriculum by extending areas of learning in the specific areas of under-standing the world, literacy, mathematical development and expressive art and design. Although these areas are apparent before three years old, it is at this age that quality interactions will support children to increase their vocabulary and knowledge.

School readiness is about preparing children to follow a set of rules, to work with each other and to learn how to become independent in their learning. It is also about school talk. Success at school depends on being able to understand and use 'school talk', a special type of talk that is used in the classroom known as 'academic talk' or 'classroom discourse' (Van Kleeck and Schwarz, 2011: 29). I remember my dad telling me that a teacher once asked him: 'What is 6 x 4?' He replied, 'Don't you know?' It was not received well!

School readiness should prepare children to understand the difference between formal talk and casual talk. Learning to respond to a question by put-ting up their hand or understanding that a teacher knows the answer but would like to see if the child knows the answer, enables the child to understand the rules of formal schooling.

The Tickell Review (Tickell, 2011) summarised school readiness as support-ing children to develop skills that they need for life. Children need to feel ready for school. For example, they need to be toilet trained, capable of putting on their coat and taking off their shoes and of listening to other children. Children are not expected to know completely how to read and write, but to have the capacity and motivation to begin to show an interest in literacy and numeracy that will support them in gaining writing and maths skills. It must be realised that some children will not be ready for school. It may be that they will always need specific help and support or they may need support for longer. Some children may not be ready for school at four years and may need more opportunities for school readiness.

If we are truly to listen to the voice of the child, this is the time that we listen to their choices, worries and what they want to say. I also believe that school readiness should not be hurried and should remain at the pace that the individual child feels secure with. I believe this is where settings may not have the scope to support their unique development. The evidence is clear that children who are behind in their development at age five are much more likely than their peers to be behind still at age seven; this can lead to sustained but avoidable underachievement.

In a reception class, a practitioner may have children that are five or are just four years old and the abilities and needs are very broad. There should definitely be a play-based curriculum to support children for each of their milestones. This is the year that teachers need to support children on a much more individual basis. Preparing children for school readiness does not mean bracketing all children into the same learning activities. Some children may need more hands-on, practical opportunities, securing a base in the prime areas of learning; some may be emergent in their literacy, ready to learn letters, numbers and words. It could be argued that there is a tendency to rush this year for many children. Many practitioners feel under pressure to ensure children are school ready; it is interpreted as a year in which they should know their phonics, key words and numbers, although they may not be school ready in terms of listening, negotiating and sharing or in their physical development. Hurried learning has a detrimental effect on children's development.

Formal schooling should not mean boring schooling. There is a great debate around the age of formal schooling. Our European counterparts do not start formal schooling until seven years old, with a much more play-based curriculum up until that age. However, it is not completely play-based. Small-group work in these neighbouring countries focuses on getting children school ready just as we do, but they have a longer time to do it. In the UK, when children start Year 1, they must follow the national curriculum whether or not they are ready for school. The curriculum dictates that at this age they should all be ready.

Every child is unique; from three to five years old, gaps emerge that influence outcomes. To reduce the gap and improve outcomes, the approach needs to be different for each child. Practitioners would have more success and achieve successful outcomes if the drive towards school readiness was slowed down and a play-based approach continued until six or seven years old, with adult-directed learning in small groups or based on individual needs. This would allow the practitioners time for quality interactions, especially with those children not able to access quality interactions at home.

The milestones from three to five years old can be achieved either very early, for some children, or very late, for others – I would suggest not until six or seven years of age in some cases.

Research from New Zealand compared children who started formal literacy lessons at age five with those who started age seven. They showed that early formal learning does not improve reading development, and may even be damaging. By the age of 11, there was no difference in reading ability level between the two groups. However, those who started aged five developed less positive attitudes to reading and showed poorer text comprehension than those who had started later (Sebastian *et al.*, 2013: 33).

It found that, around age ten, children learning to read at seven had caught up to those learning at five. Later starters had no long-term disadvantages in decoding and reading fluency. For whatever reason, the later starters had slightly better reading comprehension. Reading appears to be built on oral language, decoding and reading skills. This research suggests some focus on teaching reading early could be relaxed.

Successful and effective school readiness prepares children with the skills to self-regulate. Through play, children become more aware of, and more in control of, their physical and mental activity. This allows them to gradually rely less on adult support and become more self-regulating intellectually and emotionally. Studies suggest that encouraging play early on enhances this ability, and that interventions supporting young children enable children to be successful in independent learning (Jess *et al.*, 2004). 'The development of self-regulation and executive function is consistently linked with successful learning, including pre-reading skills, early mathematics and problem-solving' (Roberts, 2016).

School readiness for three- to five-year-olds needs a curriculum that provides ample opportunites for quality interaction, a curriculum that allows children to develop self-regulating skills and a language-rich environment where children have opportunities to see and hear language. It also needs practitioners to make the child's learning visible to all who are supporting the child. Ensuring each child's learning is reflected and supported in the best way for that child will lead to a more successful and achievable true school readiness.

Milestones

Milestones for three to four years old include:

- speaks easily without having to repeat syllables or words;
- uses sentences with four or more words;
- talks about activities at pre-school or friends' homes;
- answers simple 'Who?', 'What?', 'Where?' and 'Why?' questions;
- questions why things happen;
- uses a range of tenses;
- can retell a simple past event;
- hears the television or radio at the same sound level as other family members;
- hears you when you call from another room.

Milestones for four to five years old include:

- pays attention to a short story and answers simple questions about it;
- hears and understands most of what is said at home and in school;
- uses sentences that give many details;
- tells stories that stay on topic;
- communicates easily with other children and adults;
- says most sounds correctly, except for a few (l, s, r, v, z, ch, sh and th);
- uses rhyming words;
- names some letters and numbers;
- the prime area of communication and language, but also the specific area of literacy comes in to play.

The practitioner reads a story to the children which begins conversations around animals, pets and caring for them. Children learn the rules of conversation. They listen to the story, knowing when to interact

Three to five years: links to the Early Years Foundation Stage curriculum

School readiness and the EYFS curriculum

School readiness asks the practitioner to support the child in routines and learning activities that he or she will encounter in school. Children will be learning from the prime areas and specific areas of the curriculum and they should be encouraged to talk and have positive interactions with practitioners that show a genuine interest in them, their skills and development.

Specific areas:

Literacy: children need to see and hear literacy happening around them. A practitioner's role is to observe so they can support next steps, but also to interact with the children.

Speaking: extend and expand on what children are saying and asking. Children may start to ask the same questions repeatedly. For example, when on a car journey, if you stop at the traffic lights because they are red, a child may say: 'Why do we stop?'

The child may ask the same question every day and the adult may give the same response: 'Because the red light means we have to stop.' Or you may say: 'Because the red light means the car has to stop to let people cross the road.' But the child's

Table 4.1 30–60 months: communication and language

Unique child	Positive relationships	Enabling environment
Beginning to use more complex sentences	Introduce new words in the context of play	Help children to build their vocabulary
Can retell a simple past event	Use lots of statements	by extending their experiences
Use talk to connect words	Show an interest in the words children use	Ensure all practitioners use correct grammar
Questioning	Help children expand on what they say	Foster children's enjoyment of spoken and written language
Uses a range of tenses	Uses talk to organise, sequence and clarify things	of spoken and written language
Uses vocabulary that effects the breadth of their experiences		Give time for children to initiate discussions and
Uses talk in pretending objects stand for something else	Introduces a storyline or narrative into their play	have conversations with each other
Early learning goal (DFE, 2014b)	Encourage rules of conversation turn-taking	Decide on key vocabulary linked to activities
Children express themselves effectively, showing awareness of listeners' needs. They use past, present and future forms accurately when talking about events that have happened or are to happen in the future. They develop their own narratives and explanations by connecting ideas and events	Show children how to use language for negotiation	Provide opportunities for talking for a wide range of purposes
	Encourage children to experiment with sound and words, e.g. nonsense rhymes	Provide opportunities for children to participate in meaningful speaking and listening activities
	Encourage language play	Set up collaborative tasks
	Value children's contributions and use them to inform discussion	
	Encourage children to predict endings of stories	

brain may be thinking much deeper than this and this one repeated question is asking for a more in-depth answer. Why do we stop? This question gives the adult the opportunity to reflect on this enquiry by asking: 'Why do you think we have stopped? Do you know how the traffic lights work?' Children are naturally curious and often, when asking questions repeatedly, what they are saying to us is: 'I want to know more about this. I want to understand about the red light. How does the red light work? How does it change from amber or green?'

The practitioner needs to have lots of statements and fewer questions

There is a need for questioning in the early years, but do not bombard the child, asking 'What?', 'Who?' or 'Where?' constantly, as this form of questioning only requires one-word responses. Rather, questioning is a skill to facilitate extending language, vocabulary and thinking.

Marion Dowling emphasises the quality of questioning and explains open questioning as the key. Children need a thinking companion, someone for the child to have extended conversations with (Dowling, 2013). Depending on the setting, this could be the key person, or childminder. Anna Craft defined open questions as possibility questions (Anna Craft et al., 2015) Statements give rise to further talk from the child, providing opportunities for long conversations. '[W]e get better at using words… under one condition and only one – when we use those words to say something we want to say, to people we want to say it to and for purposes that are our own' (Holt, 1967: 124).

Practitioners need to consider what activities provoke children to discuss, chatter and ask questions.

Philosophy for children

Questions that encourage children to think can be added to the day. For example, 'Can you have a chocolate teapot?'

The chocolate teapot is an example of how to encourage sustained thinking and conversations at home and continue into the classroom. Children's philosophy lessons can be fun and interesting. Giving a child a question to discuss at home and chat about in the setting may give rise to many long conversations that, in turn, can be developed in writing and reading. This activity allows children to form opinions, listen to and respect the opinions of others and understand the rules of discussion.

Emergent writing

Children will write if they have an interest in what they are writing about. And they will write about their experiences. If their experiences are sparse, then writing may not flow as easily. They will come to the book corner if they have had opportunities to listen to books at home. The voice of the child now needs to be fostered in literacy. Experiences for children will determine their confidence in literacy. Practitioners need to find out if the child has books at home or can go to the library. The practitioner needs to reflect on what effective writing opportunities they provide for children in their care:

- Does the child have opportunities to experience visits to different places?
- Has he or she walked in the forest, been to a farm or had a trip to the seaside?

Being pulled around the shop with no speech or interaction is not a positive experience for a child. Practitioners need to plan activities where they can talk to parents and children about their trips, visits and experiences, building in to their planning opportunities for these experiences. Writing should also be part of the day; the practitioner could have a conversation with the child as they write or draw. Children begin to realise that writing conveys a message and it consists of letters that make words. Everyone prefers to write about what interests them and this is the same for children, so practitioners need to talk to children and find out what engages them.

Emergent reading

Story-telling needs to be part of the routine of the day as much as snack time. Children can retell events or stories that they have heard or been told. This helps them to understand a story structure by the practitioner asking what happened next or what happened at the end. It gives them the opportunity to explain and use new vocabulary. It helps them to think critically.

A language-rich environment

This does not mean an environment crammed with posters from floor to ceiling but one where language is included in the daily activities. A language-rich

environment can be found in the role play area – for example, food labels within the home corner, signs for shops, books that are accessible and someone to read books with so that children understand print corresponds with spoken language and how print works.

A language-rich environment includes using the role play area

Reading leads to talk about letters and sounds. Rhyming books are excellent for this activity as children will finish off the rhyme and they will form an awareness of sound to prepare them for reading. Some lovely examples of literacy activities in a setting are show and tell, golden time and book sharing.

A conversation with Buxton Bears pre-school, Chingford: providing a language-rich environment

Carole Spraget, educational consultant and owner of Buxton Bears, reflects on how the staff at Buxton Bears pre-school in Chingford, east London, provide a language-rich environment.

At Buxton Bears, we seek to support language at every opportunity and all our planned activities promote 'key' words. These words can easily be led by staff, such as engaging children at their level and using language throughout the activity, enabling children to experience first-hand how new words can be used. Children hear and absorb; then they are able to explore these words in their own responses – for example, a sewing activity may use new words such as thread, sew, stitch, wool, hold, feel or they may be words such as pulled, pulling, pull... all words that may not be used daily but are good extensions to a child's vocabulary.

From entry to our setting, children need to feel that they are listened to, from registration – where a child is encouraged to share news – to choices and opinions throughout the session, where children are encouraged to voice their own ideas. It is important that staff can listen and respond appropriately to each individual child – for example, if language is unclear, saying no when the answer should be yes can be very upsetting for a child and may lead to that child becoming withdrawn. In this situation, it is important that a staff member helps the child to express themselves using language and gestures so that the child doesn't feel ignored. A child will not continue to attempt language, explore and extend their skills unless he/she feels confident, secure and has a developing understanding of their own self-worth.

Opportunities for language development don't need to be planned. At Buxton Bears we have several casual 'chat times' a week, which entails small groups of children and their key person spending five to

(continued)

ten minutes just sitting and talking. This can be about the day's events or anything else that the children would like to talk about; it's a simple activity that requires no planning or expected outcomes, but the key person can gain valuable knowledge on their key children's abilities – from language to personality – and their general progress and well-being. We also have daily stories, songs and role play activities where language is promoted in a way that children have many opportunities to join in repeated refrains and explore new sounds and words. As their skills develop and their confidence builds, there is no stopping a child from talking; this is the foundation to a child's development across all areas of learning throughout their school life and on into adulthood.

Students need good role models as practitioners for them to understand how to engage children in activities through quality interactions and to realise that they are part of a language-rich environment.

Verity is completing her Level 3 qualification in early years. One of her tasks is to plan for an activity that promotes healthy eating.

She decided to plan an activity around snack time. Children would often come to the table and conversation seemed to be very limited. Verity found a poster with lots of fruits and vegetables and put it down on the table. One child asked: 'Why is that there?' and others started to point and identify some of the fruits. Some fruits the children did not recognise, such as lychees and pomegranates; they began to talk about trying these fruits at

(continued)

the nursery. They also talked about the size and shape; Verity pointed out the seeds in the fruit and the seeds on the outside of the strawberry.

The poster remained on the table for fruit time and other adults would come to the table and ask about the poster. This way they could record what the children had learnt and retained about the fruits. Most of the children remembered the names of the fruits that they didn't recognise and some remembered about the seeds on the strawberries. Verity used this as an opportunity to extend conversations further by asking about the seeds and growth. Children need opportunities to talk, converse and learn through informal conversations.

Sustained shared thinking does not need planning; it often comes from everyday conversations, but by a practitioner really thinking further and deeper, a child is thus enabled to think and ask further and deeper questions.

Summary of the chapter

School readiness involves children achieving milestones that may sometimes be rushed to the detriment of the child. School readiness is an area that needs careful consideration. If we are truly listening to the voice of the child, we need to understand the need to view every child as unique and realise that some children may need more support in the prime areas of learning and interactions with practitioners in smaller groups so that they can be successfully ready for school. School readiness is not only about emergent literacy or mathematical development. It is also concerned with being physically and emotionally ready for school. School readiness also involves enabling children to understand the formalities of school.

5 | Active listening

This chapter reflects on how successful effective listening is portrayed in the setting and explains strategies a practitioner may have in place. It explains the role of the practitioner, how to engage and include parents and how to display the ways a setting is listening to their youngest children. The chapter defines active listening, considers the meaning of sustained shared thinking and reflects on the characteristics of effective learning that enable successful active listening.

Previous chapters have focused on the stages of development when considering the voice of the child. This chapter concentrates on the voice of the child as a voice that has an opinion, has choice in their own play and learning and needs to be listened to by parents and practitioners alike.

Active listening is a key skill in the early years environment. As a practitioner and even as a parent, I find myself finishing off sentences or completing problems because I may need to get lunch ready or the routine says it is time for tidying up.

Recently, my daughter brought a new bed from Ikea and she asked her friend to help her build it! 'Disaster waiting to happen,' I hear you say. 'IKEA! Flatpacked furniture! Instructions to follow! And two 18-year-olds with a hammer!'

I have built many beds from Ikea in the past and was about to jump in when I heard the dialogue, the negotiating and – yes, at times – the frustration in their conversation. I left them to it and they built the bed. What is more important is they felt so good that they had achieved this on their own with very little upset.

Active listening is allowing children, and indeed adults, time to think, to take ownership of their learning, to explore and to problem-solve. It means allowing children not only to talk and converse, but also to listen and enabling them to decide and negotiate and to give them time to use their thought processes. It also means that practitioners need to know when to listen, when to gently intervene and when to step back and let the learning flow.

Research carried out by Bergen (2002) indicates there are many connections between cognitive competence and high-quality pretend play. Children need opportunities to have dialogues with themselves when they engage in imaginative play, creating a story and giving a voice to the different characters in the story. Less verbal children may talk more during imaginative play than in other settings. 'Complex and multidimensional skills involving many areas of the brain are most likely to thrive in an atmosphere rich in high-quality pretend play' (ibid.).

Opportunities for active listening can be achieved throughout the day, but it does mean that a setting needs to reflect on their skills of communication and learning to successfully achieve active listening. Active listening is effective when practitioners build quality interactions with children in their care and with parents and carers, engaging them in their child's learning. Children's confidence will be raised and self-esteem promoted if they are truly listened to.

For example, when planning a focused activity to support language, practitioners need to ensure every child can be listened to and given opportunities to talk. According to the guidance *Every Child a Talker* (The National Strategies Early Years, 2008) practitioners need to ensure that:

> groups include a mix of children, with a range of language levels. In this way, you can show practitioners how you respond effectively and sensitively to children at different levels of language and ensure that every child takes part in the conversation.

Active listening involves listening to the wishes of children

'Spending time with children, talking to them, and making sure that you are actively listening and taking seriously what they say is an essential safeguarding activity'.

(Dalzell and Chamberlain, 2006)

This list has been compiled by children to explain what they would like to happen in a setting:

- get to know us – spend time with us and give us your attention;
- don't get us to retell our story repeatedly;
- keep us at the centre of the decisions you make;
- be honest with us and explain in a way we can understand;
- let us make some decisions about our own life;
- don't make assumptions about our thoughts and feelings.

Ibid.

Active listening also involves observing and assessing children, and all staff working together to improve outcomes for all children in their care.

'Make Children's Learning Visible' (MCLV) is an observation and assessment tool that involves parents and children in learning and assessment. Pen Green Research draws on the work of Joseph Tobin (Tobin *et al.*, 1989), which presents a unique comparison of the practices and philosophies of Japanese, Chinese and American pre-school education and discusses how changes in childcare both reflect and affect larger social change. It advocates that video reflection on a settings ethos and pedagogy will help to improve outcomes and to narrow the gap between the most disadvantaged children and those that are better off.

The Pen Green Centre (2017) summarises the process into four strands for success:

- *Image of the child*: staff teams construct their 'image of the child' through dialogue and discussion on their aspirations for children in their setting – for example, they reflect on the curious child or a child with resilience and ask what do they most value and want to support in children's development and learning?
- *Pedagogical reflection through video*: staff teams reflect on video clips and discuss which aspects of their 'image of the child' can be observed in their practice.
- *Pedagogical reflection through peer observations*: staff teams observe each other and use a framework to analyse their pedagogy and ethos.
- *Assessment data collection and analysis*: drawing from rich qualitative formative assessment data detailing children's learning and development over time with parents, early childhood workers make a summative professional assessment judgement against early years outcomes in each aspect of each area of learning within the EYFS at three points in the year (September/October, January/February, May/June). Workers decide whether the child is emerging (E), developing (D) or confident (C) in each age band for each aspect, irrespective of chronological age.

The setting then devises a policy and framework within the setting that captures a child's learning journey.

Examples of good practice to enable children's learning to be visible could include a framework or policy that records the child's learning journey. This can be successful by practitioners:

- allowing children to fill out pages in their own learning journals – this gives children the opportunity to express something that interests them or something they are proud of and enables, again, another nonverbal way of having a voice;
- observing and recording their behaviour and experiences;

- asking other professionals for their knowledge of the child or young person, as they may have significantly more contact with the child;

- recording how rapport has been built with children and young people and the activities you have done together – relationships matter;

- gathering feedback from children and young people throughout an intervention – not just at the end;

- keeping children and young people appropriately involved in a realistic way – age and stage needs to be considered;

- demonstrating an active interest in the child or young person's life – their views, aspirations, interests and activities – and undertake those activities with the child;

- identifying what is important to the child or young person;

- drawing a picture of the child or young person's day to capture what it is like;

- feeding back from the child or young person on the value of being included and involved is essential. This can also support professional and practice development;

- recording the journey travelled, as the beginning and end of a child's development in a class or group are important and need to be planned for. Observation and assessment of young children needs to involve parents and carers, as well as children, in their own learning and decisions.

Active listening at its best is sustained shared thinking

Talking to children can often happen unexpectedly and doesn't fit neatly in to pre-arranged routines or activities. I always remember, during tidy up time, a child was stacking the bricks; when the bricks were stacked and he had made a tall tower, they fell. He was getting quite frustrated and it would have been much easier and quicker to tell the child go and sit down and for me to tidy up. At the time, I had a young nursery nurse who had a great quality of patience with young children; before I could jump in she said to him: 'Oh, why does that happen every time?' The young child looked at all the bricks on the floor and explained to her that every time he nearly finished, they all fell. She continued the conversation, 'How do you think we could stop it falling over? Shall we try a few bricks at a time?'

He started to stack up to six bricks and then realised it didn't topple over. A light seemed to go on in his head and he decided to put another six bricks next to the first tower of bricks. He began to talk through his action out loud and the practitioner listened, sometimes commenting, sometimes repeating his words, praising him, keeping the flow of conversation going by asking questions such as: 'What will you do next?' or commenting on his actions, saying, 'That's a good idea!' and 'What made you do that?'

Practitioners also need to learn the skill of stepping back and not saying anything or waiting for a short while before commenting, to give the child opportunities to talk more about the process and to give rise to further consideration of how buildings 'stay up', giving their own explanation. In this case, the practitioner listened. She made some notes on the conversation and his interest in buildings.

Yes! He was late joining in with the nursery rhymes at carpet time, but the dialogue and learning that took place between the practitioner and child taught me a valuable lesson. Learning is not confined to structured times. Learning opportunities take many forms and children need time to work things out to make sense of the environment. It makes them feel very confident and gives them a skill to approach learning with a sense of trying to find a solution rather than feeling frustrated and giving up. Listening – and by that, I mean truly listening and allowing the child to talk – gave rise to such learning.

A couple of days later, when it was tidy up time, I spotted him showing some other children how to 'tidy up the bricks'; he gave clear instructions. They started to ask questions about how houses are built. And so, conversations led to topics on buildings, foundations and materials that houses are made of.

> 'Sustained shared thinking' occurs when two or more individuals 'work together' in an intellectual way to solve a problem, clarify a concept, evaluate an activity,

extend a narrative etc. Both parties must contribute to the thinking and it must develop and extend.

Sylva et al., 2004: 36

It is something that we should be doing naturally; talking to children and allowing them to talk, and allowing them at times to lead the conversation and the thought process. Vygotsky's theory of the 'zone of proximal development' describes the gap between what a child can do alone and what they can do with the help of someone more skilled or experienced, who could be an adult or another child.

The gap does not always have to be filled with questions. Vygotsky defines the gap, this zone of proximal development, as a potential time for children to work out their thought process by talking to the practitioner, talking to their peers or talking to themselves or by pondering and quietly working it out. We need to give children space to do this as, when opportunities are available for children to transfer knowledge, they learn to make links with other situations and that is when sustained shared thinking has been successful.

The EPPE project (Sylva et al., 2004) was the largest study in Europe of preschool care and education. It measured the quality in early years settings and identified what made a good-quality provision and what was considered effective. It found that, from observing children's language, dialogue and adults' questioning techniques, the more we allow children to think and truly enter into a dialogue with them, the more effective their learning.

Active listening and positive body language promote good communication

Starting conversations is a good example of sustained shared thinking. From playing 'peek a boo' with babies to introducing new and interesting objects to toddlers, conversations can emerge. Hiding an item and allowing the children to discover it enables some open-ended questioning to begin.

Vivian Gussin Paley explains that we need to allow children to tell their own stories as, from this, so much more learning unfolds. Providing children with a language-rich environment as early as possible will help to develop their voice in the environment. Environment print walks are a good way to start getting children to explain and talk about what they can see.

We need to record and observe children's dialogue in their role play and their creativity to understand the child's thinking and support it. Active listening may be something a practitioner considers during planned activities such as story time. Opportunities should be made available to share a book throughout the day with children. A practitioner may share a familiar book with a child during a one to one interaction. If a practitioner decides that they want to share a book with a larger group, then it is important to consider what learning is taking place. Reading a story opens many opportunities for conversations, but conversations cannot be held within a large group. Quiet children will remain quiet, chatty children may take the lead. It is not enough just to contain a large group while lunch is being prepared or at the end of the day before the arrival of parents.

Examples of active listening in the environment

- A speaking wall that displays 'wow' words, enabling children to use these words in their routines and activities. Parents may share words that children have used at home on this wall.

- Listening walks: opportunities provided by listening walks mean that practitioners can build up a picture of the vocabulary of children.

- Let the home corner speak to the child. The home corner can be extended to support talking – for example, adding utensils that make the children ask what it is, how it works. Also, rooms can be added to a home corner and other sections made – for example, you may have a home corner and a shop and a bus or car made from chairs that shows a journey from the home corner.

- Cause and effect toys. Give children toys that they can take apart and put together – for example, an old telephone. Having conversations with them and asking them how they think things work gives rise to further conversations.

- A reading corner is also a speaking corner. Books with puppets and props enable children to understand the beginning, middle and end of a story and to understand the characters in a story. They may use different voices or tones when retelling stories; they may tell each other stories.

- Set aside time to talk: ensure children have time to talk and someone to talk to, especially children who may not have those opportunities at home or have speech delay. Observe children. Ask parents who the child talks to at home.

Practitioners need to ask themselves:

1   What can the children hear?
2   What can they see?
3   What can they touch?
4   What can they smell?

Examples of active listening in the wider environment

Opportunities for outings in the local area and perhaps further afield provide opportunities for active listening.

1   Have the children in our setting been to the seaside?
2   Have the children in our setting been to the forest?

The more a child does, the more child sees, the more a child responds. Examples of activities that children could encounter on their journey may include:
feeding the ducks, going to the shops, going on a walk in the forest or going to a museum.

   Embrace dislikes – do not tell a child they are wrong for having a dislike; however, promote a positive attitude towards such things. For example, it is okay to not like playing outdoors; however, it is good for us to get exercise to stay healthy.

Well-resourced and accessible areas enable children to express their interests and to have a voice through choice

This does not have to mean expensive toys and resources.

The cardboard box in the setting

Leave a cardboard box in the middle of the room and allow children to design what they want. Listen to them, observe how they work together.

Circle time and show and tell

Allow the children to create their own agendas for the circle time session. This will enable them to express themselves and to create their own conversations. Show and tell is a nice way to give children a voice and encourage the quieter children to join in with group conversation and to have a voice.

Symbols or picture cards

These can be used as choice cards at the beginning of the session to show what activities they would like or for various times of the day, such as choosing a song they would like to sing. This is a great way of giving children a voice, even if they don't have the language to support their own voice.

Box of children's interests

Having a box for children's interests or observations on planning shows you are considering the child's voice.

Celebrating culture and beliefs

Celebrating cultures and beliefs shows children that they are valued and that they can express their thoughts and feelings about who they are and what they believe in.

The characteristics of the EYFS of active learning, thinking critically and play and exploring should enable children to speak and be listened to.

Giving children a choice is essential in the early years and this is reflected through the EYFS documents. Not only does it support best practice and show you are promoting the EYFS outcomes, meeting Every Child Matters outcomes, but it also shows you are addressing children's rights. Allowing children to have a voice is stated as a basic right by the United Nations, highlighting the importance of giving children a voice.

This promotes self-esteem and self-worth. By giving children a voice through choice, opinion, feelings and emotions, children can develop and learn that they are important and valued. Feeling valued plays a large role in how a child learns. For them to play and explore, actively learn and critically think, they need to feel confident in their environment and have the knowledge that their voice and way of exploration will be noted.

An enabling environment actively encourages and offers children the opportunity to play and explore. By exploring and playing, the voice of the child becomes vocal. It is heard in the explorations, asking why, how, what if? Children are more interested in attempting a task if it is of interest to them. Therefore, adults should tune into children's interests. Creating an environment that is led by children's interest will encourage children to become active learners. It will also help practitioners identify and plan the children's next steps. Knowing the interests of the child means asking the child, allowing them to be part of the planning process. Practitioners need to provide children with lots of opportunities to work things out on their own; as children begin to engage fully in activities, they will start asking questions about how things work. At this stage, adults need to be skilful in asking open-ended questions or, as Anna Craft describes, posing 'possibility questions' (Craft *et al.*, 2015) to help extend the learning opportunities.

Active listening: a skill to be learnt and fostered

Having knowledge of child development is imperative for practitioners to be successful, but even more important is having a workforce that knows how to engage and interact with children so that they build on their confidence, develop problem-solving skills and learn through play and exploring: ultimately, the characteristics of effective learning. This demands practitioners to be competent in listening to the voice of the child in their care – and to actively listen. The essential ingredient for this to be successful is to have a high-quality workforce. The *Nutbrown Review* highlighted a quality workforce as one of the key factors that enable children to develop successfully (DFE, 2012). Active listening is a key skill that practitioners need to learn and to share with each other, involving parents and children in the learning process.

Summary of the chapter

Active listening is a key skill in ensuring that the voice of the child is heard. By allowing children to be part of the planning process, children's interests are promoted in activities and routines. When a child is involved in something that they are interested in, they will be more vocal and more

(continued)

enthusiastic in their play. There are many examples of how active listening can be promoted, both in the indoor and outdoor environment, often with resources that enable children to use their imaginations to be vocal.

For active listening to be effective, practitioners need to engage and interact with children and have training that ensures they are competent in the many ways that they can listen to the voice of the child.

The hundred languages of children

6

Listening to the varied voices of a child

This chapter will look at effective strategies when listening. It will consist of examples of good practice and will explain how practitioners can listen and communicate with children, supporting their individual needs through using different communication methods. By listening to the voice of the child, a child's well-being will flourish and grow.

The chapter will consider how a practitioner can be a good listener and give examples of listening activities and opportunities for listening in daily routines.

Practitioners all know how important active listening is to support a child in his or her development. Practitioners understand the importance of the variety of ways children can express their voice, and yet pressures and stress seem to squash the many ways children can express themselves.

Practitioners need to listen to children and provide opportunities that allow the voice of the child through many activities and experiences that children take part in. Children express themselves in many ways and there are a 'hundred languages of children'. Children express themselves through role play, dance, art, signs and gestures, as well as speech.

The Good Childhood Report of 2016 compares children's subjective well-being in the UK and other countries using surveys that included over 28,000 children and young people aged eight to 17 years. It found that well-being was an extremely important part of a child's development, and that it has an effect on other outcomes in life such as physical and mental health. Matthew Reed, Chief Executive of the Children's Society charity, stated that nearly 10 per cent of children in the UK experience low self-esteem and well-being and need support (The Children's Society, 2016).

The report summarised the fact that children are happy with four aspects of life:

1   relationships with people in their family who they don't live with;
2   money and possessions;
3   friendships;
4   local police force.

However, it showed that children in the UK have relatively low levels of satisfaction with four aspects of life:

1   their relationships with teachers;
2   their body;
3   the way that they look;
4   their self-confidence.

In the early years setting, it has been realised that the prime areas are fundamental to a child's overall successful development. As practitioners, we need to spend time on personal social and emotional development, as well as communication and language and physical development to ensure the foundation of their learning is built on self-confidence, self-awareness and managing feelings. To be a truly effective listener, practitioners need to make eye contact, getting down to the child's level, and start conversations relating to things that the child wants to talk about. Practitioners need to reflect on the skill of questioning. It is not enough to identify a child's interest; practitioners need to challenge and extend thinking around interests.

An effective listener understands that children express their voice through many channels. The area of expressive art and design gives a child a voice. Through music, art, drama and movement children express their feelings and emotions. Emotional well-being is essential for children's development and allowing children to express themselves through these mediums is a positive way to support their voice.

An effective listener:

Intervenes only when necessary or to move on conversations

Models activities or speech rules

Provides opportunities for children to talk and converse

Reflects on their practice

Observes children to support next steps

Values contributions from parents, other professionals and children

Interacts with children, especially children who may have very few opportunities for interacting with adults at home

Supports all children in their care

Evaluates their practice constantly, involving children in the process

Activities such as mindfulness and yoga can be firm foundations and, hopefully, can support the children identified as needing to improve their well-being.

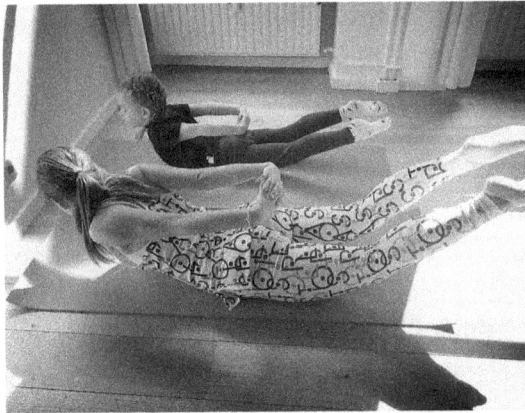

From my own experiences, I have been fortunate to see the positive impact of both these enlightening and reflective initiatives for all children and for a range of ages.

Recently, at a secondary school where I was teaching, I was asked to give a lesson on mindfulness. I used the 30-minute slot in the morning during 'form time' to present the idea of self-reflection. The age ranges were from 11–17 years old. My idea was to take a simple 20 minutes out of the lives of the young people to engage with an object, in this case a raisin. It is an activity that many mindfulness teachers use. I asked them to hold the raisin, smell it, touch it and gain an awareness of its relevance. As a recently new teacher of mindfulness, I was not confident with the task; however, all of those students lapped up the opportunity just to sit and relax. In fact, feedback after the lesson, was very positive. Most of the students commented that they never, ever just stop. They wanted to do the lesson repeatedly.

Children have so many pressures on them today to do well, to succeed and to gain the best grades. Along with this, children have the added stress and anxiety about growing up. The findings from *The Good Childhood Report* (The Children's Society, 2016) show that children worry most about how they look and relationships.

The NHS web page promotes mindfulness under how to alleviate stress, anxiety and depression. Mark Williams, professor of clinical psychology at the Oxford Mindfulness Centre, says, 'Mindfulness means knowing directly what is going on inside and outside ourselves, moment by moment' (National Health Service, 2016).

From my first lesson, it came to light that the students found there was so much to remember, so much to cope with; sometimes, they didn't know how or who could help or even felt embarrassed or ashamed to ask for that help. From that lesson with the raisin, I was enabled, as a form tutor, to just sit and be aware. With more time set aside for mindfulness, students began to interact positively with each other and myself.

This activity may seem miniscule, but it has a huge power to interrupt the 'autopilot' mode we often engage day to day, and to give us new perspectives on life. It is a mechanism that I have adopted in my own life. As a teacher, lecturer and early years inspector, pressure and stress is constantly in one's life. Teachers are continually reflecting on their day and the children in their care.

I don't think any teacher or practitioner that I know ever finishes their job at 3.30; summer holidays are often used for planning and preparing. We do have to reflect on how this stress not only impacts on our lives, but also on the lives of the children we teach.

If we want to support children in developing a good self-esteem about themselves and gain an emotional intelligence, then we, as educators, also need to take time to consider our own self-esteem and ways of promoting that and alleviating stress. Sometimes, just taking a breath may help to slow down the treadmill that we seem to never get off.

For younger children, we also need to be aware that we, as practitioners, should be building up their self-esteem and confidence from a very early age. From very young, we want children to play alongside each other (16–26 months, according to EYFS personal and social and emotional development). Building up a child's self-confidence and self-esteem enables them to have positive relationships in their lives.

We are asked to support children to feel good about themselves and their own achievements for them to be successful. We want children from a very young age to have a good sense of well-being because we know that will help them to develop good self-esteem and confidence that will contribute to their overall development.

How can we help and support our youngest children? Through observing the effect in a real-life classroom, to reading articles on mindfulness and yoga, it is evident that this should be positively reinforced within the daily routines of young children's lives.

Case study

Clair-Louise, founder of The Yoga Tree
(see: http://theyogatreelux.com/classes)

Clair-Louise has started to offer yoga classes to young children; her lessons are successful and encourage confidence, self-esteem and fun. She believes that children are natural yogis and spoke to me about why she felt yoga was a good initiative to promote well-being. She described yoga as 'flexible, fun, but most of all enlightening'.

She explained that:

> As we grow up, the world around us influences the people we become. Our world is beautiful and many of the experiences that affect us are positive. But there are also the negative pressures that often determine our state of being. We can't escape the reality of the problems that life may throw our way but we can develop an attitude towards them that allows us to cope with the bad days a bit better. Like with everything, change starts with the individual and, although the smaller beings in our world may have been around for less time than us, it is them who our focus should be placed upon.

(continued)

It is true that in today's world, most children are over-protected. It is a parent's worst fear that their children may be harmed, so we teach children the lessons we feel they need to learn to survive as it is vital that they know how to look after themselves. But the question I often wonder about is: are we forgetting about the child's instinct to love and connect?

I believe that it is vital for children to develop an emotional intelligence for them to think and create critically. You cannot have one successfully without the other. 'Emotional intelligence is the ability to perceive, reason with, understand, and manage emotions. Doing so enables us to develop and maintain productive relationships with others' (Decker, 2017).

But, just as we need support to develop our cognitive skills, we need support to develop our emotional intelligence and I feel that mindfulness and yoga can be successful in enabling children to achieve this well-being and so ensure that they can learn. We need practitioners and parents to be supportive in activities and experiences that allow children time to grow and build their own self-worth.

Getting parents involved means that the child can understand the importance of such an activity.

The Reggio Emilia approach explains that we are facilitators; parents, as well as practitioners, need to facilitate their child's learning. It advocates that the learning can take many forms and describes children's communication as the 'hundred languages of children'. Dance, music and art, but also mindfulness and yoga are just as important as mathematical development, literacy or science. This positive association with learning can lay the foundation for an enjoyable journey of education throughout childhood.

Yoga for children is not about producing perfect yoga poses or about being the best; it's about being a child and enjoying all aspects of childhood. This goes for the adults too! Grown-ups have a habit of getting caught up in adulthood and they forget about breathing out and having fun. Practising yoga as an adult is all about getting to the core of who you are as a human and about being in touch with your inner self without inhibitions or worries. Children are a perfect example of this state that we strive for. Yoga provides an opportunity for children to teach their parents about the importance of finding their inner child.

A conversation with Clair-Louise Walsh, founder of The Yoga Tree in Luxembourg

Children and family yoga classes focus on partner work, group work and extending the act of human connection beyond the comfort of our family units to others around us. Clair-Louise believes that, as a teacher, yoga classes for children provide her with endless opportunities to encourage love, light, kindness, courage, sharing, compassion, acceptance, laughter and fun into people's lives and, as a direct result, her life is also full of such positive energy.

Every week, parents and children come together in a little studio in Luxembourg and a yoga class unravels a story. This week, Clair-Louise explains:

> We practised our warrior pose, saluted the sun, picked up feathers with our toes, encountered some scary sharks under the sea, met a French mermaid, tried some acrobatics with our mums and dads and had a lovely little snooze and snuggle at the end.

The mantra of every class is sung at the end of the session: 'I am bountiful, I am blissful, I am beautiful in every way, exhale, exhale, I am fearless today.'

Case study

Music and the voice of a child

A dedicated music teacher, Carmel Burke has worked in many schools across Warwickshire and the West Midlands and believes that music is a great way for children to find their voice. She explains that music is a wonderfully creative subject for children who find it difficult to express

(continued)

themselves. Playing an instrument gives a child the opportunity to perform when, perhaps, a speaking role might be too daunting for them.

A child may be happy to perform on a musical instrument or to sing or dance and this allows adults/teachers to see them in a different light. For a child who finds it difficult to communicate with people in everyday situations, music provides a less threatening environment for communication. A child who learns a musical instrument develops in confidence; it provides a means of self-expression.

Music in the classroom can bring out a more positive attitude in a pupil who may, in general, find social interaction difficult. Engaging with music can be a very happy and positive experience for a child who is usually reluctant to put themselves forward in class.

Art and language: a perfect combination

Art is another area in which children find their voice. Through painting and drawing, through creating, children express their thoughts and feelings. Art can be a useful tool to enhance a child's speech and language development. Art therapy and speech therapy both share similar components related to language and expression, such as expression with tone of voice and body orientation. Art therapy is a form of communication development that allows individuals to express themselves using visual mediums. Individuals are encouraged to talk about their artwork and asked to share with others what they are working on. This allows an opportunity for a child to gain self-confidence and build their self-esteem.

By using art, children may have the opportunity to talk about what they are creating and practitioners can ask the child a variety of questions about the craft, targeting specific grammatical structures in instructions or recall.

Role play

The role play area gives children an opportunity to re-enact their understanding of the world. Imaginative play is a crucial component of a child's normal development. What may seem to be a simple and uncomplicated way for children to entertain themselves is a complex process that affects all aspects of a child's life. Play shapes how children make sense of their worlds, how they learn thinking skills and how they acquire language. So how does imaginative play boost a child's brain development? How can it affect cognition? There are a multitude of ways in which unstructured, child-centred play builds healthy minds. Children have dialogues with themselves when they engage in imaginative play. Role-playing means creating a story and giving a voice to the different characters in the story. When children imitate others, they are developing a vocabulary that allows them to name and navigate the world around them. Less verbal children may talk more during imaginative play than in other settings. Children at play are making sense of the world through a process of 'inner speech' – that is, they often talk out loud to themselves.

Movement: physical development and its role in emergent literacy

Movement is our first language. It is the way we express ourselves. It helps us get from A to B or turn our head and reach out our hands to show that we want something. The brain's primary purpose is to organise complex movement as this enables us to make sense of our world. Movement and physical development is vital for learning, and child-led physical play is a vital part of early development and learning. Physical play also keeps children healthy and boosts self-esteem. Children need to run around, skip, jump and climb from a very early age, not only for their confidence and to encourage independence and risk-taking, but also because it prepares them for the fine motor skills they will need for school.

The UK chief medical officer has issued guidelines known as *Start Active, Stay Active* (Department of Health, 2011). It states we should aim for at least three hours of opportunities for physical development in the early years across every day. Examples of such physical activity include jumping, climbing, skipping, throwing, catching, walking, messy play, object play, tummy time, dance and games. The guidelines encourage us to make 'every movement count'.

The UK has just enjoyed the Olympics in Rio 2016 and achieved a great number of medals in a variety of sports, and yet our children seem to be inactive and rising obesity is a serious problem among the youngest members of our society. Children are gripped by a 'crisis of inactivity', says Baroness Campbell, Chairman of the Youth Sport Trust and former head of UK Sport. She warns that schools must play a bigger part in tackling a this crisis among children (Campbell, 2014). 'The costs of physical inactivity are plain for all to see – childhood obesity levels continue to dominate the headlines, and we know that being inactive increases the risk of developing a host of other chronic conditions' (ibid.). She refers to children as being 'physically illiterate' because of the reduction of time playing outdoors, and continues to comment that an active child also will perform better academically.

There is a link between literacy and numeracy skills and physical development. The way a child holds a pencil or is able to sit and focus on activities stems from the physical opportunities that they have hopefully encountered to acquire these skills. The success stems from the strength of the foundations.

Sally Goddard Blythe has carried out research and adds that physical inactivity also has consequences on literacy and numeracy. She calls for an assessment of children's basic physical development at five years old and recommends screening children for basic physical problems at five, saying developmental difficulties can have a major bearing on later academic results. Basic screening should be introduced to identify pupils who lack the fundamental physical attributes needed to take part in lessons (Goddard Blythe, 2012). Goddard Blythe, Director of the Institute for Neuro-Physiological Psychology in Chester, said the tests were needed because large numbers of children with basic developmental problems were 'slipping through the net' (ibid.).

Assessing children when they start school enables a practitioner to gain an idea of their literacy and numeracy levels and these assessments continue throughout primary and secondary school. In fact, so much emphasis is placed on children's attainment targets in literacy and numeracy, they often lead to stress and pressure. And yet, by carrying out some simple assessments in physical development, as Goddard Blythe recommends, it may help cancel out the stumbling blocks some children have with literacy or numeracy.

There was a clear link between poor physical coordination in primary school and performance in literacy and numeracy tests taken at the age of 11. Research has suggested as many as half of children have an underlying problem with undeveloped physical skills (ibid.).

By placing emphasis on children's physical development, it should be considered that physical coordination, balance and good posture is needed before the start of school to allow children to develop the fine motor skills required to hold a pencil in lessons.

Why is there little emphasis on physical play? In fact, many schools have set playtimes and children are often expected to sit at desks from a very early age when, perhaps, they should be walking around and exploring during their learning. 'If basic physical skills are underdeveloped, children are going to struggle with independent learning tasks' (Paton, 2014b).

The skill of writing seems to be a concern with many primary school teachers. Children tend to have difficulty and their handwriting is often illegible. Writing is a physical skill. Children learn to manipulate a tool. If the physical side of writing proves difficult, the creative side of writing often takes a backward step as children may become frustrated or give up with the skill before their imagination can flow from the pages. Mechanical barriers may hinder a child's ability to pass information from the brain, through the body onto paper.

> It introduces a mechanical problem in the action of writing, which may just interfere with how much a child writes or what their handwriting looks like. But in some cases, it can also interfere with the ability to think and write at the same time; to express thoughts in written form.
>
> Ibid.

It is important to identify what Goddard Blythe refers to as 'soft signs', which are indicators that enable us to see where problems may occur. Tests should include:

- being able to stand on one leg;
- being able to stand upright for several seconds while opening and closing their eyes;
- walking along an invisible straight-line heel to toe.

Pupils who struggle the most can be given simple physical exercises to enable them to reapply the reflexes and physical coordination they should have picked up as toddlers. Without these attributes, many young people lack the physical maturity needed to support skills such as balance, hand–eye coordination, the control of eye movements needed to read and even the ability to sit still.

The work of JABADAO has as its underlining ethos to promote learning through physical play. It was established in 1985 and displays on its website the desire 'to create more opportunities for people of all ages and energies across the UK to be exuberantly and physically playful because it has the potential to make life so much better' (JABADAO, n.d.).

Between 1998 and 2009 the organisation researched and created developmental movement play (DMP), which they define as an approach putting 'movement play' on the map for early years children and influencing thinking about the importance of physical play in child development. DMP is now widely used across the UK.

JABADAO reflects on the developmental stages of physical play.

The necessity for physical activities in the EYFS

Tummy time

A baby should have lots of time on its back or 'tummy time' to build foundations for comfort, strength and ability. Early movement helps the brain to develop agility.

Upright runners

Two-year-olds are 'upright runners'; we must be careful not to rush children. Floor play is hugely important here and we should not focus too much on children sitting at tables.

Sensory play

Children need lots of sensory physical play to support balance and coordination. By having this, it will make concentration and sitting at table top activities more effective in the long term.

Physical skills

Time needs to be set aside to enable children to acquire skills such as throwing, catching and doing up zips and buttons, but it is vital that they have a whole-body spontaneous physical play. School readiness needs purposeful movement built in to the planning of play, just as much as emergent writing and emergent maths skills play, and – because of this essential factor – physical play should not be confined to 15-minute playtime.

Plan for physical play opportunities every day

It really is very simple. Plan for physical play is as important as planning for literacy or maths if we want children to be ready for school. They need opportunities to run, skip, jump and climb and they need to acquire skills such as balancing and coordination as it supports focus and concentration. If they have difficulty writing or concentrating, then practitioners need to look for the soft signs and be alert to how they can plan for physical activities to help build up the skills needed.

Children develop larger muscles of the trunk and arms before they develop the smaller muscles of the hands. They develop muscles closer to the body such as the shoulder and upper arms before the ones that are further away. And, by building up these muscles, children's writing skills will become easier to support. Practitioners need to give children opportunities to use these muscles. Children need to stretch, carry objects, throw, catch.

A wonderful teacher I worked with would start his lessons with a throwing and catching activity. The children were building up these muscles before writing and he also found the concentration proved better. Brain gym is a fantastic example of enabling children to move physically in order to concentrate and focus longer.

We need to make time for children to run around, jump, skip and play outdoors around a big area, not just confined to a small garden or playground. And practitioners should join in. We need to be role models for children in our care. We need to run with them, we need to play skipping games with them. Some schools and nurseries go for walks to local parks, where the children can run around. Many schools have initiatives such as walk to school or walk a mile every day after lunch. We also need children to learn to manage risks as this builds up their skills to problem-solve and work things out.

Expressive art and design in the early years curriculum and opportunities for speech

Table 6.1 Early years art and design

Area Expressive art and design	Opportunity for speech and hearing the voice of the child
Exploring and using media and materials	In this area of development, children express themselves through a variety of mediums. This is their voice. The pictures that they draw, the music that they make expresses who they are, how they are feeling, what they want to say
	Practitioners need to allow children to express themselves in this way but need to converse with them about their pictures, music or play. They need to be involved in the child's learning
Early learning goal	**Examples of activities to enhance the voice of the child through expressive art and design**
Children sing songs, make music, dance and experiment with ways of changing them	Learning the words to songs, familiar nursery rhymes
	Making up their own songs and practitioners learning the words to these songs
Children safely use and explore a variety of materials, tools and techniques, experimenting with colour, design, texture, form and function	Opportunities for rhyming, alliteration, discovering the patterns of sounds
	Listening to music that the children enjoy listening to dancing to traditional and popular songs
	Knowing the names of instruments and the sounds that they produce
	Allow children to lead movement sessions based around their interests
	Encourage children to talk about what they want to design, paint or sculpt
	Demonstrate and teach skills and techniques and talk about these techniques
Being imaginative	**Plan imaginative experiences, using stories to re-enact the story movement**
Children use what they have learnt about media and materials in original ways, thinking about uses and purposes. They represent their own ideas, thoughts and feelings through design and technology, art, music, dance, role play and stories	Explaining their ideas
	Expressing themselves through different media
	Using descriptive language
	Communicating though their bodies
	Using imaginary words
	Provide stimulus for their imagination

Summary of the chapter

The voice of the child can be expressed through a variety of media. Art, music, yoga and mindfulness illustrate to the practitioner that children have several ways of expressing themselves. These ways also support children to do so in a manner that will, hopefully, ensure they do not get frustrated in using their voice. It gives them the ability to use their voice in a calm way. The voice of the child may be demonstrated in the movements or music listened to, it may be in the art or designs created and these areas of development need to be apparent in the early years curriculum as much as literacy and numeracy.

7 The child's voice as a participant in the community

The child's voice is a key element of the democracy and individual liberty aspects of British values. The common inspection framework has responded to the voice of the child by ensuring that the child's voice reflects the ethos of the setting. One of the main points that the new common inspection framework asks practitioners to consider is the views of children, starting with the very young. This is recorded in the self-evaluation form (SEF) of the setting.

Children should have the opportunity to share their ideas about the setting and learn from the very start how their voice is important in the wider community. They have the right to participate and learn how to become responsible citizens. This chapter explains how children can participate in the setting and community, and why it is important. It addresses the need to give a voice to our young children so that they feel part of their environment.

Giving children a voice in the setting

When evaluating the success of anything, the most essential question to ask is whether the provider is delivering a successful product to the client. In the case of early years, first and foremost, practitioners should be asking themselves:

1   Are we delivering a successful and effective curriculum to the children in our care?
2   Do they feel valued and respected?
3   Are they involved in the planning and are their interests and needs built in to the activities and routines?
4   How do we know that we are doing our best for every child to achieve?
5   Are we enabling children to become responsible citizens and feel part of a community that cares about and embraces their opinions?

The answers to these questions demand the voice of the child to be clearly heard in the setting and recorded in such materials as the SEF. The answer will also be evident in how children learn and can achieve through observations and assessments.

A good setting will provide opportunities for children to be heard. Displays in the setting should demonstrate how children's interests are taken into consideration. Conversations with parents and carers should indicate how a setting engages with the family of that child to achieve the very best outcomes.

But to be truly successful and effective in hearing the voice of the child, the early years practitioner should equip all children with the skills for their voice to be heard as they grow and develop and realise that they are part of a much bigger voice. Their voice is as one of the participant in the wider community. Listening to the voice of the child from an early age enables the child to grow up feeling part of a community and part of a democracy. It promotes their self-esteem and self-awareness, so that they are free to make choices, but have a deeper understanding that with choices comes responsibility.

Further questions arise:

1   Are we giving children skills for the future that enable them to be a responsible member of a society?
2   Are we supporting them effectively so that they become good, caring, responsible citizens?

Table 7.1 Early years approach to citizenship

Citizenship	Early learning outcomes	Positive relationships	Enabling environment
Managing feelings and behaviour	Children talk about how they and others show feelings They work as part of a group and understand and follow the rules They adjust their behaviour to different situations	Talk about fair and unfair situations Model being fair – for example, when choosing children for special jobs Children will know that they will be listened to when they raise injustices	Plan small group or circle times when children can explore feelings Provide activities that require give and take or sharing Use persona dolls to support children in considering fair ways to share
Self-confidence and self-esteem	Children are confident to try new activities and say why they like some activities more than others They are confident to speak in a familiar group They say when they need help or do not need help Support children to feel good about their own success	Talk to children about choices that they have made and help them to understand that this may mean they cannot do something else Ensure that the key practitioners offer extra support to children in new situations	Plan future activities and experiences for each child Consult with parents about children's varying levels of confidence in different situations Provide opportunities for children to talk to about something that they are interested in
Making relationships	Children play cooperatively, taking turns	Help children to understand the feelings of others	Create areas where children can sit and chat with friends

(continued)

Table 7.1 Early years approach to citizenship (continued)

Citizenship	Early learning outcomes	Positive relationships	Enabling environment
	They show sensitivity to one another's needs and form positive relationships with adults and other children	Plan support for children who have not made friends yet Continue to talk about feelings Model ways of noticing how others are feeling and comforting or helping them	Provide resources that promote cooperation between two children Plan activities that require collaboration Provide stability in staffing

Source: DFE, 2014b

Responsible citizens

The curriculum guidance for the foundation stage identifies the following aspects of learning which underpin citizenship:

* self-confidence and self-esteem;
* making relationships;
* behaviour and self-control.

The EYFS curriculum gives ample opportunity for the voice of the child to be heard. The table above sets out the area of personal, social and emotional development where practitioners support children to be confident and resilient in their development, equipping them with the skills to communicate and express their needs, be supportive of others and learn to resolve conflict, negotiate and compromise. These qualities will have a positive impact in the future if they are fostered and supported from an early age.

Investing in time to enable children to find their voice and know how to express their voice in a meaningful, responsible way is paramount to a successful generation that knows how to listen, how to negotiate and how to resolve disagreements. This will enable children to feel part of the wider community. It will also enable children to understand democracy, which is 'a shared belief in fairness and equality and a right to participate in important decision making' (Sargent, 2016: 15).

By understanding the aspects of democracy, the voice of the child forms the voice of the wider community and demonstrates an understanding of fairness, equality, participation and shared responsibility.

The voice in the wider community

Children must have a sense of belonging in the wider world and a knowledge of how the world works. They need, from an early age, to be taught to respect each other and work together to create and be part of a positive community by making constructive relationships with each other. Global citizenship is an awareness of the links between the local and the global. It aims to foster skills and attitudes which enable children to have a positive impact on the world, in the belief that they can make a difference. Building empathy, appreciating diversity and learning skills such as how to resolve conflict, negotiate and compromise are all key to this approach. Global citizenship acknowledges our responsibilities, both to each other and to the earth itself. By giving children a voice in the early years, in effect, practitioners are giving them a level of responsibility that is key to their growth into responsible citizens.

Global citizenship is as relevant to foundation stage children as it is to older children and adults. The role of global citizenship education is to:

- help children to overcome their differences in fair and non-violent ways, laying the foundations for how they will deal with conflict and related issues in later life, enabling them to contribute positively to society;
- learn to admit to and learn from mistakes, which can, in later life, help to foster a belief that things can be changed for the better and that individuals can make a difference in the world;
- gain a positive sense of their own identity through seeing positive images of themselves in relation to others and others in relation to themselves.

Lea, 2011

Ultimately, the role of citizenship is to think critically, solve problems and express opinions. Giving a child a voice from an early age enables them to develop this into a responsible voice, by developing self-awareness and self-confidence, learning how to play and work well with others and recognising his or her place in the wider community.

Links to British values

By enabling children to participate in the wider community, practitioners are ultimately promoting the British values of:

Democracy, which can be defined as a right to participate and focuses on shared responsibility. The early years needs to provide opportunities for children to understand fairness and equality, share responsibility and participation.

Fairness and equality can be developed through circle time activities where children take turns to speak and are encouraged to listen. Children also need to be part of the rule-making process for their group and have opportunities to play games that have rules that are followed. Practitioners that mediate and help children to resolve conflict in a responsible and fair way are teaching those children how to resolve conflict as they grow and develop.

Individual liberty entails freedom of choice and freedom of expression, but with this right comes responsibility; teaching children how to express their views and opinions in a responsible way is a skill that most adults still need to learn. Practitioners should celebrate individuality and support children in managing risks, realising that mistakes are part of the learning curve. This is where settings can truly give children a voice by participating in the local community.

Rule of law By teaching children from a very young age about behaviour and consequences, by enabling children to think for themselves and understand why something was wrong, we are giving them the skills needed in the future to be a responsible citizen. Young children feel reassured in a positive secure environment, so regular routines allow children to cope better and feel safe. The most successful rules are where children have taken ownership of these rules and feel part of the process.

Mutual respect and tolerance Finally, the responsible citizen is one who respects, tolerates and understands. Young children should be given the knowledge and experience of the cultures within their community in order to ensure discriminatory attitudes are not part of their future. Welcoming the many faiths, customs and beliefs in a setting and community enable families to feel welcome and valued.

A successful setting will strive for 'an inclusive and cohesive learning community' (Sargent, 2016) that nurtures a generation to be responsible, caring and actively positive citizens.

Self-esteem goes hand in hand with the importance of collaboration and working together. The many voices of children can impact the wider community and world of tomorrow. Even from a very early age, young babies are actively seeking to develop relationships with parents or carers by turn-taking during early communication and the use of gestures, expressions and body language to engage with the world around them. As they grow from infant to toddler to foundation-age child, their interaction with the world blossoms and grows. During this phase 'they are constantly re-evaluating their "sense of self", and, therefore, their social and emotional competence and their ability to establish meaningful relationships with others' (Gandini and Pope Edwards, 2001).

When referring to the role of the practitioner, it is essential to realise that the way that adults talk to each other will impact on how children believe is the appropriate way to talk to each other. 'How adults speak to one another, to children and to parents, how they listen and display curiosity and interest, and how they handle conflicts, underpin all the different interactions and activities that take place in the setting.' (Telfer-Brunton and Thornton, 2004).

If we want children from a young age to grow into responsible citizens, then practitioners, parents and adults within our community and the wider world also need to be responsible citizens in listening to children in our care. A society has as much responsibility to care for children as parents and, therefore, legislation and policy need to reflect how we listen to our younger generation.

For practitioners to be effective, they need skills such as advocacy, empathy and effective listening to truly hear the voice of the child. Advocacy is defined as the act of someone speaking on behalf of someone else to influence decisions based on the best interests of that person. In the case of a young child, a practitioner and parents and, indeed, a community should be advocates for that child, to strive for the best environment and create positive relationships with all involved.

Listening to the voice of concern

It is imperative that practitioners listen to the voice of the child when that child has a concern or worry. It is also essential that children are equipped with the skills to deal effectively with bullying and learn to be assertive: to say when they are unhappy with the way that someone is behaving towards them.

The UNCRC lists the rights of all children; children should have a means to express their fears or anxieties if they feel that their voice is not heard. A practitioner's role is to ensure that the views of children, who may have difficulty expressing their voice, are echoed and repeated through the practitioner.

Many children today have been victims of extremely difficult experiences that have impacted on their self-esteem, their self-worth and their resilience. Adults need to find a platform for their voice. Many charities advocate this by allowing children to tell their story, to recall their experiences, to deal with them and move on. For example, The Children's Society relates stories from child refugees or asylum seekers in the hope that these experiences will diminish if their plight is told and listened to.

An enabling environment

Providing an enabling environment from an early age and advocating individual liberty, ensures children are given a voice that is meaningful and valued.

Having a sense of right and wrong is vital for children so that they are more likely to feel secure in the choices that they make. Empowering children enables them to feel confident in their voice. This can lead to freedom of speech, but it must be noted that children need to be able to listen to others, as opinions affect how others think and feel. This leads to children understanding differences of opinions.

For children to be confident in free speech, they need opportunities to access a learning environment that encourages speaking skills.

Checklist of good practice to support the voice in the wider community

The *Every Child Matters* green paper of 2003 insists that practitioners listen to the voice of the child and believes the five outcomes are the success criteria to demonstrate this listening (DFE, 2003).

The five outcomes are:

1   being healthy;
2   staying safe;
3   making a positive contribution;
4   enjoying and achieving;
5   economic well-being.

The key to economic well-being is a positive attitude, success in learning and emotional intelligence.

Involving children in local campaigns such as fundraising or recycling

The *Good Childhood Report* summarised the fears and worries that children have in their community and what makes the feel safe (The Children's Society, 2016). Practitioners need to ask children what they like about where they live, what they dislike and what they would like to change. One of the five outcomes of *Every Child Matters* (DFE, 2003) is for children to make a positive contribution. This should include encouraging children to support the community and environment, engage in positive behaviour both inside and outside of school, develop self-confidence and successfully deal with significant life changes and challenges.

Many settings now fundraise for charity or donate food to the elderly or those in need, perhaps from the harvest festival. Children need to understand that being part of a community entails caring for those around us. Becoming responsible citizens means taking care of our community and, indeed, our world.

Practitioners could build in to their planning opportunities for children to choose a charity to support and get them to help publicise it. They could join initiatives that demonstrate how to take care of the community – by recycling or picking up litter. Posters displayed in the local shops on the high street or in the library could show how children are involved in their community. Many settings have campaigned for cars to drive slower on busy roads where schools are built – children's artwork is displayed on lamp posts asking drivers to slow down.

It is important for children to understand that this is their community and that their voice will be heard.

Listen out for the interests of the children and incorporate the interests in to the environment

The interest of children is paramount to effective learning. Children will learn when they have an interest in what they are learning, so practitioners need to listen to the child, find out their interest and nurture this interest. For example, practitioners could foster creativity and introduce children to art and artists, encouraging them to have an opinion and asking them what they think is their favourite art or music or poem.

Ensuring the wider community listens to the voice of the child

This demands that the community listens to the voice of the child and needs to consider the following:

1   Is there accessible transport to and from settings?
2   Are there homes that provide shelter and a warm and safe place for children to grow and develop?
3   Are there areas for children to play and explore in a safe way?

Summary of the chapter

During the early years, listening to the voice of the child enables children's social development, helping them to engage with others, to develop understanding of their communities and society – thus providing opportunities for responsible and active citizenship. Children are the future generation and will have us as their role models to learn how to behave towards each other. Therefore, the practitioner, parent and adults within the community need to be positive and responsible in their interaction towards each other. Children also need to learn about the wider world and the importance of caring for each other and the world that we live in.

The *Every Child Matters* document (DFE, 2003) that led to the Children Act 2004 demanded that every child had a right to be healthy, stay safe, enjoy and achieve, make a positive contribution and enjoy economic well-being. For this to happen, the voice of the child needs to be listened to and children need opportunities to participate in decision-making.

This can be achieved by involving children in local campaigns, fund-raising for charities, listening to their interests, fostering their learning and ensuring the wider community listens to the voice of the child.

8 Concluding thoughts

To truly listen to the voice of the child, we need to be patient, understanding and invest our time in all they do and say. Theoretical perspectives reflect on the importance of the voice of the child in their learning and development. A child who is positive and confident as they grow will become competent and resilient in their lives.

Child development plays a key role as the stages of development help practitioners understand the needs and interests of children in their care. By understanding child development, practitioners need to support each child in their care by listening to the expressions of the child. This starts from birth. Crying is the beginning of the voice of the child and a voice that needs to be listened to and acted upon. 'The workers need to find the confidence and listen to this appropriate crying and not try to hush it up, allowing the child to use their voice' (Goldschmied, 2003).

It must be considered that the voice may sometimes be silent, but it is essential that, even during quiet times, the voice of the child is visible in their demeanour as this is an expression of their voice. Practitioners need to know the children in their care well. They need to create an environment that enables children to communicate their feelings and preferences, and support them in expressing these feelings. Partnership with parents is essential, as sharing information around routines and needs will make learning effective and successful.

Practitioners need to be active listeners, engaging with children, motivating them and enabling them to learn the skills of creating and critically thinking through stimulating communication. This can be achieved through a variety of ways that the Reggio Emilia approach defines as the 'hundred languages of children'.

Finally, the voice of the child is one aspect of British values – namely democracy – that acknowledges their voice, allows them choice and encourages them in their decision-making, supporting them to be valued members of their community.

Ultimately, children should be free to make their own choices, voice personal opinions with a responsible attitude and have a sense of identity and belonging without fear of discrimination. To have an effective voice, children need to have a self-awareness and self-belief as it helps them to care for others rather than having poor self-esteem, looking outwards and hurting others.

The voice of the child needs the practitioner to actively listen and enable the child to express their voice through a variety of areas in the EYFS. The voice of the child may be silent but expressed through music, art and movement. Active listening is crucial as children who feel that they are listened to will be confident and self-assured.

References

Bandura, A., Ross, D. and Ross, S. A. (1963) Vicarious reinforcement and imitative learning. *Journal of Abnormal and Social Psychology.* 67(6), pp. 601–7

Barr, R. (2013) Memory constraints on infant learning from picture books, television, and touchscreens. *Child Development Perspectives.* 7(4), pp. 205–10. Available at: http://onlinelibrary.wiley.com/doi/10.1111/cdep.12041/abstract (accessed 27 June 2017).

Bergen, D. (2002) The role of pretend play in children's cognitive development ECRP. *Childhood Research and Practice.* 4(1). Available at: http://ecrp.uiuc.edu/v4n1/bergen.html (accessed 27 June 2017).

Berwick, R. and Chomsky, N. (2016) *Why Only Us: Language and Evolution Cambridge.* Cambridge, MA: MIT Press.

Boundless (2017) *Bandura and Observational Learning.* Available at: https://www.boundless.com/psychology/textbooks/boundless-psychology-textbook/learning-7/cognitive-approaches-to-learning-48/bandura-and-observational-learning-203-12738/ (accessed 27 June 2017).

Brotherson, S. (2009) *Understanding Brain Development in Young Children.* Available at: https://www.ag.ndsu.edu/pubs/yf/famsci/fs609.pdf (accessed 27 June 2017).

Bruce, T. (2012) *Early Childhood Practice: Froebel Today.* London: Sage.

Bruner, J. (1983) *Child's Talk: Learning to Use Language.* New York: Norton.

Campbell, S. (2014) *Schools Play Key Role in Tackling 'Crisis of Inactivity'.* London: Youth Sport Trust. Available at: https://www.youthsporttrust.org/news/schools-play-key-role-tackling-crisis-inactivity (accessed 17 July 2017).

CDM Child Development Media (2017) *Play: The Work of Lev Vygotsky*. Available at: http://www.childdevelopmentmedia.com/articles/play-the-work-of-lev-vygotsky/ (accessed 27 June 2017).

Chalmers, D. (2017) *Communicating with Children from Birth to Four Years*. Oxford: Routledge.

Chomsky, N. (1965) *Aspects of the Theory of Syntax*. Cambridge, MA: MIT Press.

Clare, A. (2016) *'Professional Love' in Early Years Settings*. Available at: https://www.pacey.org.uk/news-and-views/pacey-blog/july-2016/%E2%80%98professional-love%E2%80%99-in-early-years-settings/ (accessed 27 June 2017).

Clark, A. and Moss, P. (2011) *Listening to Young Children: The Mosaic Approach*. 2nd edn. London: National Children's Bureau (NCB).

Craft, A. (author), Chappell, K. (compiler), Cremin, T. (compiler) and Jeffrey, B. (compiler) (2015) *Creativity, Education and Society: Writings of Anna Craft*. London: Trentham.

Daly, M., Byers, E. and Taylor, W. (2006) *Understanding Early Years Theory in Practice*. Portsmouth: Heinemann, Pearson Education.

Dalzell, R. and Chamberlain, C. (2006) *Communicating with Children*. London: National Children's Bureau.

David, T. (2004), Show the way. *Nursery World*. Available at: http://www.nurseryworld.co.uk/nursery-world/news/1089918/show-the-way (accessed 27 June 2017).

Decker, D. (2017) *Transition Times Critical Thinking versus Emotional Intelligence: Which Wins?* Available at: http://qualitytransitions.com/critical-thinking-versus-emotional-intelligence-wins/ (accessed 27 June 2017).

DFE (Department for Education) (2003) *Every Child Matters*. Available at: https://www.education.gov.uk/consultations/downloadableDocs/EveryChildMatters.pdf (accessed 27 June 2017).

DFE (2012) *Nutbrown Review: Foundations for Quality*. Available at: https://www.gov.uk/government/publications/nutbrown-review-foundations-for-quality (accessed 27 June 2017).

DFE (2014a) *Early Years Pupil Premium: Guide for Local Authorities*. Available at: https://www.gov.uk/guidance/early-years-pupil-premium-guide-for-local-authorities (accessed 27 June 2017).

DFE (2014b) *Statutory Framework for the Early Years Foundation Stage*. Available at: http://www.foundationyears.org.uk/files/2014/07/EYFS_framework_

from_1_September_2014__with_clarification_note.pdf (accessed 19 July 2017).

Department of Health (2011) *Start Active, Stay Active: Report on Physical Activity in the UK*. Available at: www.bit.ly/startactive (accessed 27 June 2017).

Dolva, G. (2009) *Vygotsky in Action in the Early Years: The Key to Learning Curriculum*. Oxford: Routledge.

Dowling, M. (2013) *Young Children's Thinking*. London: Sage.

Edmunds, F. (2004) *An Introduction to Steiner Education: The Waldorf School*. London: Sophia.

Fenson, L., Marchman, V.A., Thal, D.J., Dale, P.S., Reznick, J.S. and Bates, E. (2007) *MacArthur-Bates Communicative Development Inventories (CDI): Words and Gestures*. Baltimore, MD: Brookes.

Gandini, L. and Pope Edwards, C. (eds) (2001) *Bambini: The Italian Approach to Infant/Toddler*. Amsterdam and New York: Teachers College Press.

Goddard Blythe, S. (2012) *Assessing Neuromotor Readiness in Learning: The INPP Development Screening Test and School Intervention Programme*. New York: Wiley Blackwell.

Goldschmied, E. (2003) *People Under Three: Young Children in Day Care*. 2nd edn. London: Routledge.

Guernsey, L. (2012) *Screen Time: How Electronic Media – From Baby Videos to Educational Software – Affects Your Young Child*. New York: Basic.

Gussin Paley, V. (1990) *The Boy Who Would be a Helicopter*. Cambridge, MA: Harvard University Press.

Hadley, P.A., Rispoli, M. and Hsu, N. (2016) Toddlers' verb lexicon diversity and grammatical outcomes. *Language, Speech, and Hearing Services in Schools*. 47, pp. 44–58.

Hagan, J., Shaw, J.S. and Duncan, P.M. (eds) (2008) *Bright Futures: Guidelines for Health Supervision of Infants, Children, and Adolescents*. 3rd edn. Elk Grove Village, IL: American Academy of Pediatrics.

Hart, B. and Risley, T. (1995) *Meaningful Differences in the Everyday Experience of Young American Children*. Baltimore, MD: Brookes.

Holt, J. (1967) *How Children Learn*. New York: Pitman.

Hughes, A. (2009) Learning and development: treasure baskets and heuristic play. *Nursery World*. Available at: http://www.nurseryworld.co.uk/nursery-world/

feature/1092689/learning-development-treasure-baskets-heuristic-play-choice (accessed 13 July 2017).

Huttenlocher, J., Haight, W., Bryk, A., Seltzer, M. and Lyons, T. (1991) Early vocabulary growth: relation to language input and gender. *Developmental Psychology*. 27, pp. 236–48.

Iverson, J.M., Hall, A.J., Nickel, L. and Wozniak, R.H. (2007) The relationship between reduplicated babble onset and laterality biases in infant rhythmic arm movements. *Brain and Language*. 101, pp. 198–207. Pittsburgh: University of Pittsburgh.

JABADAO (n.d.) http://www.jabadao.org/ (accessed 27 June 2017).

Jess, M., Dewar, K. and Fraser, G. (2004) Basic moves: developing a foundation for lifelong physical activity. *British Journal of Teaching Physical Education*. 35(2), pp. 23–7. http://www.research.ed.ac.uk/portal/en/publications/basic-moves-developing-a-foundation-for-lifelong-physical-activity(13fce3db-8bea-4f44-a791-d0f8ff937e0f)/export.html (accessed 19 July 2017).

Knight, S. (2016) *Forest School in Practice*. London: Sage.

Lea, K. (2011) *It's Good to get Global! Global citizenship in the Early Years*. Early Years Foundation Stage Forum. Available at: http://eyfs.info/articles/_/early-years-general/its-good-to-get-global-global-citizenship-in-r69 (accessed 27 June 2017).

Lowry, L. (2013) *Making Sure Children Get Their Daily Dose of Language Nutrition*. The Hanen Centre. Available at: http://www.hanen.org/Helpful-Info/Articles/Making-Sure-Children-Get-Their-Daily-Dose-of-Langu.aspx (accessed 27 June 2017).

Mann, D. (2013) *Babies Listen and Learn While in the Womb*. Available at: http://www.journal-news.com/lifestyles/health/babies-listen-and-learn-while-the-womb/Noirw7oBgCJnKnNppq7zLK/amp.html (accessed 27 June 2017).

Malaguzzi, L. (1996) *The Hundred Languages of Children*. Translated by Gandini, L. Catalogue of © Preschools and Infant-Toddler Centres: Istituzione of the Municipality of Reggio Emilia, Italy: Reggio Children.

McGillion, M., Herbert, J.S., Pine, J., Vihman, M., dePaolis, R., Keren-Portnoy, T. and Matthews, D. (2017) What paves the way to conventional language? The predictive value of babble, pointing, and socioeconomic status. *Child Development.*. 88(1), pp. 156–66.

Montessori Primary Guide (2017) *Introduction to Sensorial.* Available at: http://www.infomontessori.com/sensorial/introduction.htm (accessed 27 June 2017).

Montessori Research and Development (2013) Listening and speaking in the Montessori Classroom. *Language Arts Manual Vol. 1: Early Years.* Available at: https://www.montessorird.com/sites/default/files/samples/MP.LA1_SP.pdf (accessed 27 June 2017).

My ECE Experts (2013–17) *ECE experts Te Whariki: What is this Early Childhood 'Curriculum' that ECE Services are Required by the Ministry of Education to Follow?* Available at: https://www.myece.org.nz/educational-curriculum-aspects/106-te-whariki-curriculum (accessed 27 June 2017).

National Association for the Education of Young Children (2017) *A Conversation with Vivian Gussin Paley.* Available at: http://www.naeyc.org/content/conversation-vivian-gussin-paley (accessed 27 June 2017).

National Health Service (NHS Choices) (2016) *Stress, Anxiety and Depression: Mindfulness.* Available at: http://www.nhs.uk/Conditions/stress-anxiety-depression/pages/mindfulness.aspx (accessed 27 June 2017).

NIDCD (National Institute on Deafness and Other Communication Disorders) (2017) *Speech and Language Developmental Milestones.* Available at: https://www.nidcd.nih.gov/health/speech-and-language (accessed 27 June 2017).

Nutbrown, C. (1994) *Threads of Thinking.* London: Sage.

Ofsted (2015) *Common Inspection Framework: Education, Skills and Early Years from September 2015.* Available at: https://www.gov.uk/government/publications/common-inspection-framework-education-skills-and-early-years-from-september-2015 (accessed 27 June 2017).

Page, J. (2015) Love, love, love. *Nursery World.* Available at: http://www.nurseryworld.co.uk/nursery-world/opinion/1152266/love-love-love (accessed 27 June 2017).

Pantley, E. (2013) *Should Babies and Toddlers Watch Television?* Child Development Institute. Available at: https://childdevelopmentinfo.com/family-living/kids-media-safety/television/babies-television/#.WKWEAvmLTIU (accessed 27 June 2017).

Parent–Child Program (n.d.) *Parent–Child Interaction is Critical to Closing the Gaps.* Available at: http://www.parent-child.org/our-method-third-post/ (accessed 19 July 2017).

Paton, G. (2014a) Children gripped by 'crisis of inactivity', says sports chief. *Telegraph.* Available at: http://www.telegraph.co.uk/education/educationnews/

10617338/Children-gripped-by-crisis-of-inactivity-says-sports-chief.html (accessed 27 June 2017).

Paton, G. (2014b) Many children 'unable to hold a pencil or sit still' at five. *Telegraph.* Available at: http://www.telegraph.co.uk/education/education-news/10974849/Many-children-unable-to-hold-a-pencil-or-sit-still-at-five.html (accessed 27 June 2017).

Reece, T. (2017) *When Do Babies Start Talking?* Parents.com. Available at: http://www.parents.com/baby/development/talking/when-do-babies-start-talking/ (accessed 27 June 2017).

Reggio Emilia Australia Information Exchange (2011) *A Pedagogy Listening.* Available at: https://www.reggioaustralia.org.au/component/content/article/59 2011 (accessed 27 June 2017).

Riddall-Leech, S. (2005) *How to Observe Children.* London: Heinemann.

Rinaldi, C. (2001) Documentation and assessment: what is the relationship? *Project Zero and Reggio Children. Making Learning Visible: Children as Individual and Group Learners.* Reggio Emilia, Italy: Reggio Children.

Roberts, L. (2016) Learn about self-regulation: the key to effective early learning. *Nursery World.* Available at: http://www.nurseryworld.co.uk/nursery-world/news/1156199/learn-about-self-regulation-the-key-to-effective-early-learning (accessed 27 June 2017).

Rudolph, J.M. and Leonard, L.B. (2016) Early language milestones and specific language impairment. *Journal of Early Intervention.* 38(1), pp. 41–58.

Rymer, R. (1994) *Genie: A Scientific Tragedy.* New York: HarperCollins.

Sargent, M. (2016) *Promoting Fundamental British Values in the Early Years.* Poole, Dorset: Practical Pre-School.

Sebastian, P., Suggate, E., Schaughency, A. and Reese, E. (2013) Children learning to read later catch up to children reading earlier. *Early Childhood Research Quarterly.* 28(1), pp. 33–48. Available at: http://www.sciencedirect.com/science/article/pii/S0885200612000397 (accessed 27 June 2017).

Sylva, K. et al. (2003) *The Effective Provision of Pre-School Education (EPPE Project), Technical Paper 10 – The Effective Provision of Pre-School Education (EPPE) Project: Intensive Case Studies of Practice across the Foundation Stage.* London: DfES / Institute of Education, University of London.

Sylva, K., Melhuish, E., Sammons, P., Siraj-Blatchford and Taggart, B. (2004) *The Effective Provision of Pre-School Education (EPPE) Project: Technical*

Paper 12 – The Final Report Effective Pre-School Education. London: DfES/Institute of Education, University of London.

Tassoni, P. (2014) *Getting it Right for Two Year Olds*. London: Hodder Education.

Telfer-Brunton, P. and Thornton, L. (2004) Little citizens. *Nursery World*. Available at: http://www.nurseryworld.co.uk/nursery-world/news/1101486/little-citizens (accessed 13 July 2017).

The Children's Society (2016) *The Good Childhood Report 2016*. Available at: https://www.childrenssociety.org.uk/sites/default/files/pcr090_mainreport_web.pdf (accessed 27 June 2017).

The National Strategies Early Years (2008) *Every Child a Talker: Guidance for Consultants, Second instalment*. Available at: http://www.foundationyears.org.uk/files/2011/10/EveryChild_a_Talker_consultants_guidance2.pdf (accessed 27 June 2017).

The Pen Green Centre (2017) *Making Children's Learning Visible (MCLV)*. Available at: http://research.pengreen.org/making-childrens-learning-visible-mclv/ (accessed 27 June 2017).

The Southern Early Childhood Association (n.d.) http://www.southernearlychildhood.org (accessed 27 June 2017).

Thornton, L. (2014) *Bringing the Reggio Approach to your Early Years Practice*. Oxford: Routledge.

Tickell, C. (2011) The Early Years: Foundations for Life, Health and Learning. Available at: https://www.gov.uk/government/uploads/system/uploads/attachment_data/file/180919/DFE-00177-2011.pdf (accessed 19 July 2017).

Tobin, J., Wu, D. and Davidson, D. (1989) *Preschool in Three Cultures*. Yale: Yale University Press.

Tovey, H. (2016) *Bringing the Froebel Approach to your Early Years Practice*. 2nd edn. Oxford: Routledge.

Van Kleeck, A. and Schwarz, A.L. (2011) *Making "Academic Talk" Explicit: Research Directions for Fostering Classroom Discourse Skills in Children from Nonmainstream Cultures*. Available at: https://digital.library.txstate.edu/handle/10877/5866 (accessed 13 July 2017).

WebMD (2017) *Baby Talk: Communicating With Your Baby*, http://www.webmd.com/parenting/baby/infant-development-9/baby-talk (accessed 27 June 2017).

Zauche, L.H., Thul, T.A., Darcy Mahoney, A.E. and Stapel-Wax, J.L. (2016) Influence of language nutrition on children's language and cognitive development: an integrated review. *Early Childhood Research Quarterly*. 36, 318–33.

Index

For Product Safety Concerns and Information please contact our EU
representative GPSR@taylorandfrancis.com
Taylor & Francis Verlag GmbH, Kaufingerstraße 24, 80331 München, Germany

www.ingramcontent.com/pod-product-compliance
Lightning Source LLC
Chambersburg PA
CBHW080426270326
41929CB00018B/3174